HAUNTED WILTSHIRE

HAUNTED WILTSHIRE

Keith Wills

For Mum and Dad

First published 2014

The History Press
The Mill, Brimscombe Port
Stroud, Gloucestershire, GL5 2QG
www.thehistorypress.co.uk

British Library Cataloguing in Publication Data.
A catalogue record for this book is available from the British Library.

ISBN 978 0 7524 9311 4

Typesetting and origination by The History Press
Printed in Great Britain

CONTENTS

ACKNOWLEDGEMENTS

I would like to express my warmest thanks to all those who have helped make this compilation possible: the publicans, the hoteliers, the custodians, the staff and volunteers at English Heritage and National Trust properties. I must also extend my heartfelt thanks to the folk of Wiltshire who were only too happy to spend time regaling me with their chilling encounters.

I would also like to thank Naomi Reynolds, Nicola Guy, Declan Flynn and the editorial team at The History Press for their help and guidance in getting this thing off the ground.

And finally, a very special thanks must go to local artist Christine Bozier for the book's illustrations, and for her support, her unfailing patience and her moments of inspiration when I needed them most. Hope the journey wasn't too crazy.

All photographs are my own except the Cross Guns inn 'ghost' photograph, used with kind permission of Roger Jones of Ex Libris Press, *Hosts of Ghosts*.

Contact the author at:
keith_wills5@msn.com

Contact the illustrator at:
petportraits1.blogspot.com

INTRODUCTION

WILTSHIRE has a unique beauty, many poets have waxed lyrical describing it as wild, romantic and enigmatic. Artists apply their craft in the hope of capturing the mood of its ancient chalk landscape. It is a magical place which has won the hearts and imagination of thousands, inspired I'm sure by 6,000 years of untamed prehistory. One only has to marvel at the mysterious trilithons of Stonehenge and the megaliths of Avebury to be reminded of prehistoric man's enduring legacy and his extraordinary achievements. Wiltshire is a county steeped in folklore, legend and hauntings. Indeed, its plethora of ghosts has gained it a reputation as being one of the most, if not *the* most haunted county in Britain.

In this book I have catalogued a few of my visits to reputedly haunted locations, the majority of which I have selected for their public access. I have included first-hand accounts from eyewitnesses where possible, plus anecdotal tales passed down over the centuries. They include: the ghostly apparition of the Lady in White, said to haunt the grounds of Avebury Manor where she has a habit of seeking out male visitors as targets for her inappropriate shoulder grabbing; the Blue Lady at the Cross Guns inn Avoncliff, who pops up all too often in the ladies' toilets; Lacock Abbey, where a hideous dwarf is said to scamper about the upper floors; Littlecote House, the scene of a brutal infanticide perpetrated by the pernicious Wild Will Darrell in 1575 and where his ghost still haunts the corridors. There is also the fearsome white cat said to stalk walkers along the 5,000-year-old Ridgeway passage and the Ash Lady of St John the Baptist church, Wroughton, said to have been the victim of a premature burial during Victorian times.

ABOUT THE AUTHOR

EVERYONE knows somebody who has seen a ghost, or so they say. A study undertaken several years ago revealed that as many as 1 in 7 Britons claim to have witnessed ghostly activity in one shape or another, and the chance of seeing a ghost has been calculated as 1 in 10. When you consider that the odds of winning the lottery are in excess of 1 in 14,000,000, being struck by lightning is 1 in 600,000 and being murdered is 1 in 18,000, then there is every chance that you and I may experience a ghost in our lifetime.

The eminent author and visionary Arthur C. Clarke once wrote, 'for every man alive today there are thirty ghosts, that is the ratio by which the dead outnumber the living'. The Earth's population is approximately 7 billion, so there is potential for 210 billion ghosts happily, or unhappily as the case may be, haunting the planet. If Mr Clarke's statistics are to be believed, then you would think we would be falling over phantoms at every turn. The explanation offered by mediums and spiritualists as to why this is not so is quite simple. We, the uninitiated are not 'tuned-in' to the spirit plain.

I have spent a good deal of my life in the pursuit of this most elusive quarry, a pursuit which regrettably has yet to yield anything tangible by way of conclusive proof – but I live in hope. My interest in ghosts and haunted houses stems from when I was a child and discovered my great-grandparents had owned a haunted pub. I would listen intently, often wide-eyed and open-mouthed, to all the stories the family would regale, stories which ultimately fuelled my interest in the supernatural. It wasn't until much later, in 1995, that I took the initiative and formed an investigative group composed of people I carefully selected for their objective open-mindedness. What followed were several years spent investigating some pretty eerie locations in Wiltshire and the South West.

I hope this book will delight the ghost hunter and prompt the sceptics amongst you to perhaps reconsider. It is not my intention to offer an explanation as to why some people see ghosts and some do not, but it's interesting to note that with all of man's advancements in the field of science, he is still no closer to understanding that which we label supernatural and paranormal.

I remain, as always, an open-minded sceptic.

Keith Wills, 2013

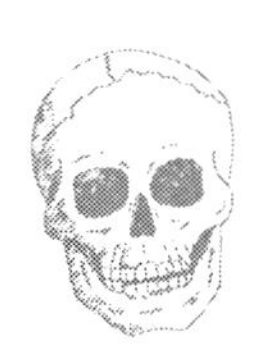

MAP OF WILTSHIRE'S MOST HAUNTED

(© Christine Bozier)

1

MANORS AND HOUSES

Avebury Manor

Avebury Manor dates from around the mid-sixteenth century, but the area the house occupies is considerably older and in all probability may have had monastic connections. There have been few excavations of note but those permitted by the National Trust have revealed finds which would indicate the area to have been occupied for at least 1,000 years.

Avebury Manor is haunted by four ghosts.

The earliest records of a building in the immediate vicinity date from 1114, when King Henry I granted the estate to his chamberlain William de Tancarville, who in that same year gifted it to the Benedictine French abbey of St Georges de Boscherville, Rouen. A priory house probably made of timber was established soon afterwards and may have stood close to where the current house is now situated. The priory was a small unit, just a few monks eking out a simple existence raising sheep and farming the land.

In 1378 England was at war with France which ultimately spelled expunction for the monks of Avebury. The last prior to leave was Stephen Fosse in 1379, one of many monks expelled from England during that year. A succession of chaplains then took charge of the priory until it finally passed into the hands of Fotheringhay College in 1411.

In 1547, following the Dissolution of the Monasteries (1536–1541), the college exchanged the estate for other lands. The Crown took possession and granted ownership to Sir William Sharington; owner of Lacock Abbey. At some point the priory was either demolished or remodelled, leaving a small lay house.

In 1549 Sharington was caught defrauding the Bristol Mint where he held the title of 'under treasurer', but managed to avoid execution by calling in a few favours in high places. He didn't get off scot-free though for he still faced a hefty fine which forced him to sell off some of his assets. One such asset was Avebury Manor, which was purchased off him by William and Mary Dunch in 1551. Evidence now points to the Dunches being largely responsible for building a new house between 1555 and 1580.

In the years that followed, a succession of owners transformed the house through major extensions and modernisation. Sarsen and limestone were used for most of the early building projects. It is likely that the sarsen stone came directly from the world-famous stone circle at a time when standing stones were of little interest other than for building material. Otherwise, the stone would have been quarried from the Marlborough Downs where it could be found in abundance.

Over its 450-year history, Avebury Manor has commanded significant importance in the village, surrounded by high boundary walls and formal gateways. Although not the most prestigious of country houses, it still retains an air of opulence with its impressive gables, deep mullion windows, tall imposing chimneys and beautiful topiary gardens.

As you might expect for a house this old, Avebury Manor has acquired quite a haunted history. It is reputedly inhabited by four ghosts, one of which is a cat, but more about him or her later. Let's start with the ghostly presence of what may be Sir John Stawell.

Sir John Stawell of Cothelstone

The staunch Royalist Sir John Stawell, purchased Avebury Manor from William Dunch in 1640. Stawell played a significant role in the English Civil Wars and raised five regiments at his own expense in support of Charles I. His allegiance to the Crown was to prove his undoing, for during one of his many campaigns in the West Country he fell foul of the Parliamentarians at the Siege of Exeter and was captured in 1646. Later that year he went to London with a copy of his terms of surrender issued by Sir Thomas Fairfax and was instructed to swear on oath 'not to bear arms against Parliament'. He refused, and in so doing was immediately committed to Ely House in Holborn on the advice that his possessions and estates were to be sequestered, which included his beloved Avebury Manor.

On 13 August 1646 he was summoned to the Bar of the House of Commons, where he declined to kneel and take the oath when ordered to do so by the Speaker. He was immediately committed to Newgate Prison on a charge of high treason. His trial took place at Somerset Assizes and was repeated several times, but on each occasion no proceedings followed. In July 1650 he was moved from Newgate to the Tower of London and on 17 December of that year he was brought to trial once more, but the judges neither acquitted nor condemned him. He remained in the Tower of London for the next eleven years. In 1652 Avebury Manor was sold to George Long who in turn leased it to Sir Edward Baynton.

Stawell was to remain in the Tower until his release in 1660 on the Restoration of Charles II. His estates and possessions were reinstated in full and he returned to Avebury where he lived a short time until his death on 21 February 1662. He was buried with great pomp at Cothelstone on 23 April of that year. Some say he died a broken man, suffering from ill health and depression. It was rumoured that he took his own life in a moment of utter despair, although there is no evidence surviving to support this claim. I suppose it is not surprising that such rumours grew as to his state of mind; heaven knows what conditions he must have had to endured during his imprisonment.

It would seem that Sir John is reluctant to leave Avebury Manor, for it is the aptly named 'Cavalier Bedroom', now the 'Withdrawing Room' (renamed for the BBC makeover in 2011) where his ghost has been seen gazing out of the south window which overlooks the gardens. He has also been spotted standing quite motionless to the left of the fireplace. He is described as being as solid as you or I in appearance, and suited in the finery of a Cavalier of the time. A melancholy figure by all accounts who, when encountered, appears to be weeping. Some say his arrival is often preceded by a sharp drop in temperature or the fragrant smell of roses, or both. The common use of rosewater as an eau de toilette could explain this; personal hygiene was yet to establish itself. Sir John is said to have adored his garden and spent a great deal of time strolling there, which may also account for reports of his ghost being seen thereabouts.

Visitors have occasionally been overcome by feelings of sadness in this room, especially standing near the south window, or 'sorrow window' as it is often called. Some have even been unable to cross its threshold, because of an intense emotional drain. Whilst I was working in the house for the National Trust, a young man in his early 20s briskly descended the exit stairs ashen-faced and visibly shaken with tears in his eyes. He asked if there was somewhere outside where he might sit. I showed him into the garden, indicated a bench seat and left him alone with his thoughts, not wishing to pry.

On returning to the exit I bumped into his parents who had followed him down. I enquired as to what the problem was and they told me that in one of the rooms upstairs he had suddenly been overcome by a deep sadness and needed to leave. I asked which room they had been in and was not surprised by the answer. I explained that there have been, and still are, many stories associated with that room and on occasion some people have felt a great sadness there. I reassured them that their son was not the first and no doubt would not be the last to experience such feelings of utter misery and dread in that room.

The Tudor Bedchamber

'The Tudor Bedchamber' is another room renamed for the BBC project. This room would undoubtedly have served as a bedchamber at some point and forms part of the east extension, built between 1580–1601. One of the house guides told me of a frightening experience he had several years ago whilst working in this room. A group of visitors had just entered, when all of a sudden one of the party, a woman, was overcome by something only she could sense:

> Her eyes rolled up till just the whites were showin' then she started to shake but worse was her voice which was all sort of deep and guttural, I couldn't understand what she was sayin'. It only lasted for a few seconds then she came out of this 'trance' I suppose you'd call it. She was led out of the room by her friends. I was told that she was a medium and she had obviously had a reaction to something in the room.

Another of the house guides will not work in this room; she too claims to be sensitive to whatever may be present here and firmly believes that this particular entity is malevolent. As for me, I love this room and it is always my first choice when I help out as a house guide. It has three large mullion windows which face east, south and west, so the room is bathed in sunlight all day long. Surely this is not an environment conducive of such a malevolent presence, but then what is?

The White Lady

The house and gardens are reputedly haunted by a beautiful young woman dressed in white. 'The White Lady' is arguably the most active of the house's ghosts and her story is one of tragedy, as are many ghost stories. Although her identity is uncertain, it is believed she may well have been a ward of Sir John Stawell.

Stawell ran a strict house, especially with regard to protecting the young lady's integrity and virtues. In defiance of these house rules, she met and fell in love with a young man who worked on the estate. Stawell got wind of her deceitfulness and immediately put a stop to their secret rendezvous. She was to have none of it and continued to meet covertly with her young suitor.

Their brief romance was to be cut short, for the young man received orders to join ranks and participate in the Civil Wars. As each day passed she would pray for his safe homecoming for they had decided to elope as soon as he returned. Then came the news that she had been dreading; her lover had been killed in active duty. With a broken heart and little to live for, she took her life by jumping from a second-floor window.

Her ghost is said to follow visitors around the gardens where she will randomly select a gentleman (preferably with a beard it would seem) and tap him sharply on the shoulder. It is believed that this 'tap on the shoulder' signifies her attempt to identify whether the recipient of her advances is that of her lover. She is most often encountered at the south gate close to the pet cemetery.

One of the National Trust guides told me of an experience he had during a film shoot whilst in the gardens. He described his encounter as suddenly being 'gripped from behind by the shoulders and pulled back'. He spun around to see who was there but to his surprise discovered nobody near him.

The White Lady has also been seen by guides and visitors descending the eighteenth-century staircase inside the house. She is dressed in a floor-length white gown and described by those who have seen her as 'stunningly beautiful'. Having said that, one of the house guides claimed to have witnessed her on the staircase, but where a head and hands should have been there was nothing. All she saw was an empty white gown gliding down the staircase.

Another story concerned a little boy of 7 who had been visiting with his parents. They had just climbed the stairs and were en route to one of the show bedrooms when they realised their son was not behind them. Just as they were about to go looking for him, he caught up with them none the worse for wear. Apparently he had been chatting happily to the 'lady in the wedding dress on the stairs.'

The White Lady haunts the grounds of Avebury Manor where her inappropriate shoulder tapping has startled many a visitor. (© Christine Bozier)

The Monk

With the house's monastic roots, it is not surprising to learn that there have been numerous sightings of a phantom hooded monk. The identity of the monk is unknown but there may be a clue as to why he haunts the house. It is well documented that in 1249 several of Avebury's monks were held at Marlborough Assizes on suspicion of murder. Could the unfortunate victim of that heinous crime be said monk?

His ghost has been seen in the kitchen, the small parlour, the east garden and the churchyard of St James, which stands adjacent to the house. One of the earliest encounters was by previous owner William Dunch. The story goes that one evening in 1557, whilst the maid was busy organising the dining room for the evening meal, she was briefly interrupted by Dunch who called to her from the kitchen. They spoke briefly in the kitchen regarding some matter or another, after which the maid returned to the dining room, stopping just short of the threshold, for, standing at the dining room table, was a 'tall imposing hooded figure'. The maid looked over her shoulder towards the kitchen where she enquired of Dunch, 'Pardon me sir! Do we have guests for dinner?' 'No!' came the reply. At that the maid looked back into the dining room to find the intruder had disappeared.

Several times a shadowy, hooded figure has been seen crossing the passage that connects the kitchen to the west garden door; a door long since bricked up.

One of the latest sightings of the monk occurred one evening as the previous curator of the Stables Museum (a building at the edge of the east garden) was locking up for the night. As he turned from the door he noticed a hooded figure standing motionless amongst the gravestones in the adjacent church of St James. The figure seemed to be looking directly at him. Thinking it to be a young local lad who had been up to mischief on several occasions near the house gates and in the churchyard, the curator decided to confront him. As he drew closer to the churchyard gate, the figure started towards him. Surprised and fearful at this sudden advance, the curator backed away from the gate, at which point the figure began to fade until nothing was left except a fine amorphous mist which slowly dissipated.

Ghostly Cat

And finally, should you venture into the Stables Museum, you will find amongst its exhibits (many of which were discovered at Avebury henge) a rather grisly desiccated cat. Said cat was apparently unearthed some years back whilst work was being carried out on one of the house's external garden walls. During medieval times it was thought that the walling up of dead cats would deter rodent infestation and keep evil spirits at bay. How times have changed – thankfully. On occasion, when staff have been locking up for the evening, they have heard the unmistakable sound of a cat crying as if locked in somewhere upstairs. When they go to investigate, nothing is ever found.

HM Prison, Erlestoke

Erlestoke House (or what is left of it, following a devastating fire in 1951 which claimed most of the house and left just two wings intact) used to stand proudly on top of a hillside at the north-western edge of Salisbury Plain. By all accounts it was a grand affair of some 365ft in length, with three storeys and a basement, the latter also surviving the great fire. Erlestoke House and Park used to dominate the little village of Erlestoke on three sides. Today it is a Category 'C' prison, housing up to 494 inmates serving sentences from a few months to life.

Erlestoke House was built between 1786 and 1791 from a design by the eminent architect George Stewart, for wealthy timber-merchant Joshua Smith. It was Smith's decision to demolish an old Elizabethan house which stood close by to make way for the new build, which was to be set in beautiful parkland with ornate bridges, lakes and waterfalls fed by natural springs. The Elizabethan house was low in the valley but Smith wanted the new house to be higher up to command an uninterrupted view across the valley. Several cottages in Erlestoke village were demolished to make way for the new house and grounds and Smith rehoused those who lost their homes in new cottages which can still be seen today. Many have strange carvings built into the walls; some are of classical figures whilst others are of grotesque gargoyles. All are thought to have been part of the original house.

Many notable guests have visited Erlestoke's two houses over the years. Queen Elizabeth I slept here in 1574. The Duchess of Kent and her 12-year-old daughter, Princess Victoria, later to be crowned queen, spent a weekend at Erlestoke in late 1830 in the company of poet Thomas More who wrote in his diary of an 'evening of music and song'. Erlestoke has also been home to several dignitaries and four distinguished members of parliament.

In 1819 Joshua Smith died and the Erlestoke estate and other lands were sold to George Watson-Taylor, a wealthy Jamaican plantation owner, for a whopping £250,000. The Watson-Taylors were greatly respected for their benevolence toward the villagers of Erlestoke; food, clothes and blankets were generously distributed by the family to the needy.

The Watson-Taylor's fortunes were to falter when in 1832 George Watson-Taylor suffered a financial setback, coinciding with the emancipation of the slave trade. He was forced to auction many of the house's treasured possessions and moved away. The house was closed for four years until it was leased to John Cam Hobhouse, later Baron Broughton (1786–1869), politician and best friend of Lord Byron.

In 1844, to the delight of the population of Erlestoke village, Simon Watson-Taylor, son of George, returned to his family home at Erlestoke. Simon was married to Charlotte Hay, and it is Charlotte Hay who is said to haunt what is now the prison, the grounds and occasionally the village.

The Ghost of Lady Charlotte Hay

A search of England's historic peerage revealed Lady Charlotte to be the daughter of Field Marshal George Hay, 8th Marquess of Tweeddale and Lady Susan Montagu. She was named Hannah Charlotte Hay at birth and was born around 1828. She married Simon Watson-Taylor on 30 June 1843 and they had two daughters, Rose Edith and Violet Emily. Charlotte died on 10 November 1887.

Lady Charlotte was personally responsible for the construction of a new church. The previous one, St James, was part of the original Elizabethan house estate and so was on her private land, and she disliked the villagers walking across her property to gain access to the church. She arranged to have St James demolished on the understanding that she commission and fund the building of a new church. The Gothic style Holy Saviour church, built in memory of her father, was completed in 1880 and cost in excess of £6,000, twice the original estimate.

There has been some speculation as to why Lady Charlotte, if indeed it is her ghost, should haunt Erlestoke Prison and its grounds. Some have suggested that she was so dissatisfied with the completed church that it kept her spirit earthbound, even though she died some seven years after its completion. I would have thought the stained-glass window in the chancel dedicated to her memory would have been enough to appease her restless spirit – apparently not.

Lady Charlotte's ghost has been seen and heard walking the basement which is beneath the prison's Education Block. She has also been seen in what remains of the old house. It may be Lady Charlotte riding a spectral horse along a road close to the house and in the vicinity of the old demolished church. It may also be her ghost that has been seen close to the spot where an ornamental bridge (long since demolished) once stood in the grounds of the new house. It is unclear whether these apparitions are of the same woman but all who claim to have seen her describe a woman dressed in grey in the style of the 1800s.

The staff at Erlestoke Prison have affectionately christened their ghost Lady Charlotte, whether it be her or not. There have been several ghostly tales reported by officers and staff claiming to have seen or heard her. Officer Grant Frost told me of an incident that happened to him:

> It was approximately 2 a.m., I had been working the nightshift. I was alone in the house which is now part of the Works Department (maintenance). I'd locked myself in as is standard procedure. I was busy catching up on some paperwork when I distinctly heard footsteps coming from the room immediately above me. Knowing full well I was the only person in the building, I immediately went to investigate but found nobody. Fully aware of the stories of the alleged existence of the ghost, I was quite content in the knowledge that the footsteps must belonged to Lady Charlotte.

The basement, once the kitchen, seems to be a hotspot for Lady Charlotte for she has been seen several times standing quite motionless thereabouts. Staff have been shocked when stepping into the basement to be confronted by her apparition; some members of staff would rather not go down there alone. I can see why the basement, with its low, arched and bricked ceiling and creepy, brooding and claustrophobic atmosphere, would unnerve many people. Footsteps, shadowy figures glimpsed from the corner of the eye, unseen hands pushing and pulling folk up and down the steps which lead to the cellars and strong feelings of not being alone or being watched are not uncommon in this area.

Littlecote House

Littlecote House (currently owned by Warner Leisure Hotels) is located within the picturesque North Wessex Downs, close to the banks of the River Kennet and the villages of Chilton Foliat and Ramsbury.

Littlecote House, once the home to the infamous 'Wild Will' Darrell.

Littlecote started life around the second century as a modest military encampment, a few rudimentary huts housing a small garrison which guarded the crossing at the River Kennet. In later years it evolved into a small farming community. A major rebuild took place in AD 120 during the Roman occupation, which included a splendid villa as its centrepiece. By the turn of the third century all farming had ceased and Littlecote had become something of a religious Mecca for pilgrims. The world-famous Orpheus Mosaic, first discovered in 1727 along with a hoard of coins believed to be that of Emperor Vespasian (AD 69–79 and founder of the Flavian Dynasty, the second imperial dynasty in Rome), was discovered by William George, a steward of the Littlecote estate. This splendid example of Roman floor decoration is regarded as one of the best preserved mosaics in Britain.

The original thirteenth-century medieval house was built by the de Calstone family. William Darrell married into the family and took Elizabeth Calstone as his wife in 1415 ensuring shared inheritance. Much later, Sir George Darrell was credited for building the Tudor mansion between 1490 and 1520, which is thought to have been the earliest brick-built house in Wiltshire. On the death of Sir Edward Darrell (son of Sir George) in 1549, his son William Darrell (also known as 'Wild Will') inherited Littlecote, but more about him later.

Littlecote has hosted several royal visits. King Henry VIII is said to have wooed his third wife Jane Seymour, the granddaughter of Elizabeth Darrell here; Henry's progeny Elizabeth I visited in 1601; King James II in 1663 and William of Orange (later William III) in 1688. The list goes on.

The current Elizabethan house was constructed by Sir John Popham (Lord Chief Justice) who bought the reversion on Littlecote and succeeded to it in 1589, following the death of William Darrell. Some say his acquisition of Littlecote was obtained by less than honest means. The new development was completed in 1592. It was Sir John Popham who presided over several famous trials, including Mary Queen of Scots (1587), Sir Walter Raleigh (1603) and the conspirators of the Gunpowder Plot, including Guy Fawkes (1606). He sentenced Mary and Fawkes to death.

Littlecote became a Parliamentary stronghold during the Civil Wars (1642–1651) and a splendid collection of Cromwellian armour survives today and can be found on display in the Great Hall.

'Wild Will' Darrell

There have been several inconsistencies with the Mother Barnes story, but after much research and stone turning I believe that what follows is a fair narrative of the events that allegedly took place at Littlecote House in 1575. John Aubrey, the English antiquarian wrote extensively toward the end of the seventeenth century and seems to be the first to have left any kind of record of the story I am about to relate. He included his account in a work on the life of Chief Justice Popham; an inclusion that would appear quite clear of detail and history.

Mrs Barnes (or Mother Barnes) was a midwife, nurse and general all-round good egg. She had no idea what horrors lay in wait for her one cold winter's night back in November 1575. In her little cottage in Great Shefford, following a particularly arduous day, she was preparing for bed when there came a loud, persistent knocking at her front door. Now Mother Barnes was used to being called upon at all hours of the day and night, such were the demands of her profession, and it was hardly rare for her to have a breathless young man in need of help delivering his first baby at any hour of the night. This night, however, the pounding at her door seemed unusually persistent; it was tenacious and urgent. Wearily, Mother Barnes went to her door pulling on her coat and collecting her bag in anticipation of yet another nightly excursion into the Wiltshire/Berkshire countryside to tend to the needs of a mother-to-be.

You can imagine her surprise when she opened the door to a mysterious man dressed entirely in black, his hat and muffle concealing all but his eyes. He quickly explained that it was in her best interests if she knew not of his identity and furthermore her services were required with much haste. He also told her that she would be handsomely rewarded for her troubles. The offer of a financial incentive was enough for her to accept, somewhat apprehensively, the stranger's request, for a midwife's profession paid little. There was one caveat though; she was to be blindfolded for the entire trip, for the location she was to be taken was none of her concern. Again she accepted, though rather dubiously. The stranger produced a blindfold, secured it about her head and then led her to a waiting horse which had been saddled for a pillion. They set off at a gallop into the night. Years later, when Mother Barnes related her story to a magistrate, she would say that she believed they had been travelling for an age but in all likelihood may only have been some 40 minutes or so. She felt sure they had left the beaten track and had travelled across field and down.

On their arrival she was led, still blindfold by her escort, into a house, up a flight of stairs and into a room. Her blindfold was then removed by her escort to reveal a sumptuous bedchamber. In bed lay a young woman whose features were concealed by a mask, but even so, Mother Barnes could quite clearly see that she was in much distress and close to giving birth. As Mother Barnes approached the bed she turned to see a man emerge from the shadows, dressed in black velvet and also wearing a mask. He told her quite curtly to be about her office and gestured impatiently toward the bed. Unbeknown to Mother Barnes, she had just encountered the owner of Littlecote House; 'Wild Will' Darrell, so named for his infamous debauchery. Mother Barnes asked Darrell if he would mind leaving the room as a birthing was no place for a gentleman but Darrell ignored her and paced agitatedly about the room. Mother Barnes thought it wise to say nothing more.

She approached the bed and tried to reassure the young woman as best as she could. Mother Barnes feared she may not survive the birth, indeed she feared for her own safety, after all, what could be less normal than being blindfold, brought to a strange house and placed in the company of a masked woman and a decidedly unpleasant masked man and then told to deliver a baby. As Mother Barnes readied herself for the task in hand, she could not help but notice the room had not been prepared to receive a newborn; there were no blankets, no water and the aging servant standing nervously in one corner did little to inspire her confidence. However suspicious Mother Barnes may have been, she complied with Darrell's wishes and within a short time a healthy baby boy was delivered. As for the child's mother, her concerns only deepened.

Cradling the infant in her apron she was about to present the child to the mother when it was taken from her by Darrell who immediately left the room, crossed to the landing and threw the newborn into the flames of a roaring fire and held it there by his booted foot. The child's screams alerted Mother Barnes who fled the bedchamber. She found Darrell at the fireplace holding the burning infant in the coals. When she saw what had happened she tried to intervene but Darrell held her back. From the bedchamber came the mother's piteous pleas for mercy, which Darrell ignored. Thankfully the child's agony was short-lived; within seconds its blistered, charred remains lay motionless in the fireplace.

Darrell grabbed Mother Barnes by the shoulders. She was now in a state of shock. He fixed her with icy, pitiless eyes and whispered through clenched teeth for her not to breathe a word of what she had witnessed tonight, for if she broke her silence then untold misery would be levelled at her door. Devastated, she asked to sit while her horse was prepared for the trip home. Darrell left the room which was just enough time for Mother Barnes to act. She raced back into the bedchamber, opened her bag and produced a small pair of scissors which she used to snip off a tiny piece of fabric from the bed hangings. She prayed this slim piece of evidence would be enough to incriminate Darrell should the authorities be able to trace the house and room from which the fabric had come.

Her escort reappeared moments later, by which time she had secreted scissors and fabric into her bag. She was once again blindfolded and led downstairs, but this time Mother Barnes took it upon herself to count the steps, again hoping her resourcefulness may help in identifying the house. When they reached her cottage (by a different route this time) she was presented with a purse of monies which she accepted. Again she was warned to say nothing of the events of that night.

Mother Barnes kept silent for years afterwards until, close to her death, she divulged all to a magistrate. She recalled everything that had happened on that night. She produced the fabric and described how she had counted the steps when leaving and also gave an approximation for the duration of her journey home. Suspicion immediately fell on Will Darrell, whose pernicious reputation was well known in the area. An investigative body was despatched to Littlecote where they examined the house and damning evidence soon transpired. The bed hangings were unchanged and the place where the fabric had been removed was soon found. The number of steps also matched the amount Mother Barnes had counted on the fateful night. This was deemed enough to charge Darrell with murder.

Darrell was committed for trial in 1586 at Salisbury, but it is thought he managed to bribe the judge, Sir John Popham, a good friend of the family. A deal was struck that if Darrell was freed then Popham's family would benefit greatly and eventually become proprietors of Littlecote. If the bribe story is true, then it worked, for it secured Darrell's release. He was never brought to trial and escaped the gallows.

Rumours grew that the poor woman who had lost her baby in such a despicable manner was that of Darrell's sister, Raquel. This theory claimed the child was a product of an incestuous relationship, a relationship that ultimately claimed her life for she is believed to have died in childbirth. However, Darrell had several mistresses, so any one of them could have been the mystery mother. Some believe the child may have been the result of a liaison with a Miss Bonham, whose brother was in service at Longleat House. Her treatment at Littlecote by Darrell was less that cordial and it was well known that she gave birth to at least one illegitimate child which sadly died.

A letter discovered at Longleat House, addressed to Sir John Thynme (1515–1580) of Longleat from Sir Henry Knyvett (1539–1598, who despised Darrell for his disgraceful activities) and written around the time of Mrs Barnes death, confirmed her story. Amongst the subject matter was condemnation of Will Darrell's scandalous activities which he is said to have perpetrated in the counties of Wiltshire and Berkshire. Sir Henry told Sir John of a Mr Bonham in his service, whose sister had become Darrell's mistress and about how the poor girl was so appalling treated at Littlecote. Sir Henry wrote: 'Mr. Bonham should be urged to do something about his sister's "usage" at Will Darrell's, what of the birth of her children, how many there were, and what became of them? For the report of murder of one of them was increasing foully and would touch Will Darrell to the quick.'

Darrell's Stile

Justice was to finally catch up with Will Darrell in 1589 when he met a violent death after falling from his horse whilst out hunting in Littlecote Park. Some say Darrell fell after seeing his murdered son's ghost suddenly appear in a flash of brilliant light. Another story, taken from one who rode with him on that day, recalls how the sunlight was particularity bright as it danced and flickered playfully through the trees, a distraction that may have momentarily dazzled his horse causing it to stumble and throw Darrell from his mount. Whatever happened on that day would seem to have left an imprint for Darrell is reluctant to leave this spot. His ghost has been seen sat astride a black stallion riding at full gallop close to where he fell, a spot referred to as 'Darrell's Stile'. His twisted figure has also been seen wondering aimlessly about the same spot, a place where many horses shy and become agitated. He has also been seen in the bedchamber and on the landing by the infamous fireplace.

William Darrell was buried on the 3 October 1589 at St Lawrence's Church, Hungerford and the Pophams inherited the estate just as the alleged bribe of 1575 had foretold. Oddly, Darrell's ghost is said to also haunt not St Lawrence but the thirteenth-century church of The Holy Cross at Ramsbury some 4 miles to the north-west. Just what the connection is, I have no idea, other than a local legend; should you be brave enough to count the hundred studs on the north door at midnight you will evoke the ghost of 'Wild Will' Darrell.

It is not surprising to learn that the room where the horrific deed took place has retained a residue. Several times over the years reports from guides and guests who have stayed at Littlecote describe the ghost of a woman who appears to be weeping whilst gently rocking a baby cradled in her arms. In 1970, a visiting journalist took a photograph of what appears to be a woman leaning over the bed. The photograph was examined by a photographic laboratory and deemed not to have been tampered with. The terrified screams of a baby have been heard emanating from the haunted landing and also the Long Gallery that runs adjacent to the bedchamber.

The ghost of a woman believed to be that of Mother Barnes has been seen kneeling by the fireplace on the landing. One would assume she is mourning the passing of a child she was powerless to save. It is also said that a blood stain occasionally appears at the spot where Darrell threw the child into the flames. Attempts to repair or replace flooring in the area because of persistent mouldering have failed, for each time work is carried out the mould mysteriously returns.

The Popham family retained Littlecote until 1922 when it was purchased by the tobacco magnate Sir Ernest Wills. During his occupation Sir Edward, brother of Sir Ernest, stayed at Littlecote with his wife. One night, Sir Edward was woken by the sound of his Pekinese scratching at the bedroom door to be let out. 'What is it boy?' enquired Sir Edward. The dog, normally obedient to his master's commands, ignored him and continued to scratch at the door. Sir Edward left his bed, opened the bedroom door and stepped out into the Long Gallery where he saw a woman dressed in pink whom he did not recognise, holding a lit candle and walking away from him. He called out to her but she either ignored or did not hear him. Curious as to her identity, he followed until he lost sight of her in the direction of his brother's bedroom. The following day he alerted the household staff and asked who this mysterious woman was. He also mentioned the incident to his brother who said he had not been disturbed that night. On overhearing the conversation, one of the housemaids stepped forward and said, 'Beg pardon Sirs, but I often see a lady wandering the Long Gallery wearing a pink dressing-gown, she is a happy ghost that means no harm or agitation to anyone.'

The butler of millionaire entrepreneur Peter de Savary (who owned Littlecote 1985–1996) was party to a strange experience in the Long Gallery during a fashion shoot for Burberry. A young model was posing by the fireplace, glancing out of the oriel window. The film crew were assembled, as were make-up artists and the woman in charge of the shoot. It is common practice to take a Polaroid snap to ensure everything is as it should be before the main shoot. As the photograph developed it revealed a great shot of the model in her evening-dress, but something else also began to appear. Standing immediately to the model's right was the figure of a woman in a white gown.

Peter de Savary went public in *Hello* magazine in October 1993 with a story so strange it beggars belief. Shortly after he had moved in, he decided to hold an auction of unwanted furniture and various other items which he had discovered in the house and had no use for. On the morning of the sale he was walking in the Long Gallery when he was suddenly confronted by a middle-aged woman dressed in a tweed suit. She spoke sharply, telling him he was a wicked man and no good would come of him unless he returned the box containing her babies' clothes that he had so wickedly removed from the chapel. A little stunned by this sudden outburst, Mr de Savary was about to ask the stranger why she was wandering about his home when she vanished before his very eyes.

Later, after recovering from the initial shock, Mr de Savary recalled the box which he had indeed quite innocently removed from a window ledge in the chapel earlier in the week. He eventually found it amongst other items for sale. When he opened the box he was amazed to find it contained babies' clothes along with papers dating to 1861. Not surprisingly, he put the box back on the chapel window ledge where he had originally found it. There were no further encounters with the woman in tweed. The box and its contents remain in the chapel today in a sealed glass case.

A phantom black dog has been seen on the 500-year-old Jerusalem staircase situated off the Long Gallery. Several years ago a visitor was confronted by said animal as he climbed the narrow staircase. As he bent to pat the dog he was stunned to see his hand pass straight through what appeared on first sight to be solid flesh and blood.

Peter de Savary's butler had another terrifying encounter whilst descending the staircase one afternoon. He had reached one particular step, often referred to as the coffin step (no idea why), when he was suddenly thrown against the wall, breaking his collar bone, shoulder and several ribs. He claims he didn't slip, wasn't pushed, didn't fall and does not drink. Although I am not doubting the authenticity of his encounter, I think it worth mentioning that these wooden steps are very irregular, uneven and could quite easily contribute to a trip or fall. That aside and assuming paranormal activity was the culprit, could de Savary's butler have been the victim of a particularly aggressive poltergeist assault?

The Woman in the Garden

One of the more frequently seen ghosts is that of a woman standing in the garden. Some years ago, one of the guides had just finished a tour of the house and gardens and was leading her party back into the house when she noticed a woman standing in the garden looking at the house. Thinking she must be one of her party, the guide called out to her to join them, but at that moment the mysterious woman disappeared. Some who have seen her claim she bears a striking resemblance to Mrs Leybourne-Popham whose portrait hangs in the Regency Room. Coincidentally, the painting shows her in the garden rather than in the house. I wonder how significant this is.

Longleat House

Longleat House is probably best known for its safari park, which includes a troop of 100 or more mischievous Rhesus Macaques whose sole intention seems to be the random destruction of your car. Amongst Longleat's many other attractions is the world's longest maze. I don't know about it being the 'longest', but it certainly rates, in my experience, as the longest time spent trying to escape from box hedging.

Longleat House lies near Warminster on the A362. It must surely be one of the finest examples of Elizabethan architecture in Britain and stands prominently in 900 acres of beautiful parkland, much of which was landscaped by Lancelot 'Capability' Brown in the 1700s. The estate was originally the site of a medieval Augustine priory, until King Henry VIII fell out with the Catholics and had the monasteries and priories and anything else that hinted at having 'monkish' connections dissolved.

During the Reformation, the Longleat estate was purchased by Sir John Thynne in 1541 for the princely sum of £53. The first house was destroyed by fire in 1567 and the second house, which remains largely unchanged, was finished in 1580 shortly before his death. It took thirteen years to complete. Longleat House has been owned by the Thynne dynasty for 470 years and the current seat is occupied by Alexander Thynne, the 7th Marquess of Bath. Longleat has become one of Britain's most visited

Longleat House, Warminster.

attractions and its safari park was a world's first when it opened in April 1966 and effectively rewrote the book on how animals should be kept in captivity.

The Grey Lady

Before I begin this story, I must make a point which will hopefully help clear up any confusion which may arise from you reading the internet and several other publications that refer to Longleat's 'Green Lady' and the 'Green Lady's Walk.' I have it on good authority, having spoken to several of Longleat's house guides, that the apparition in question is actually referred to as the 'Grey Lady' and the 'Grey Lady's Walk,' respectively. 'Why don't you call her the Green Lady?' I asked. 'Simple!' came the reply, 'She dresses in grey.' You can't argue with that.

The most famous of Longleat's ghosts is that of Lady Louisa Carteret, who married the 2nd Viscount of Weymouth, Thomas Thynne in 1733. He agreed for her to bring her own serving staff to Longleat as part of their wedding arrangements. Unfortunately, one of her entourage was a young footman whose adoration for his lady seemed to go beyond what was expected of his post, or at least that is how it appeared to a few of Longleat's household staff. They grew jealous of what seemed to be favouritism by Lady Louisa towards this young man. Rumours and suspicions grew as to the likelihood of there being extra-marital liaisons between the two. These rumours were quite untrue as it turned out, but word got back to Thomas that his wife was having an affair. Thomas was well known for his quick temper and confronted the fellow at his earliest opportunity. This happened to be in a passageway outside the old library on the first floor, beside a spiral staircase. An altercation took place and Thomas accused the footman of indiscretions toward his wife, accusations which were flatly denied. Thomas lost his temper and pushed the footman down the stairs in a fit of rage. The footman broke his neck in the fall.

Thomas, afraid of being implicated in the murder, quickly had the body buried in the cellar and told Lady Louisa that the footman had left without word. She was fully aware of her husband's distrust for her servant and did not believe him. She suspected her husband had imprisoned him somewhere inside the enormous house and spent many days and nights frantically searching every room; those that were locked she demanded be opened. But her search proved fruitless, for she never found him. It was on one of her nightly searches in the bitter cold that she caught a chill which developed into pneumonia. Lady Louisa, much weakened and distressed by her husband's deceit, succumbed to her illness during childbirth and died in 1736 at the age of 22. She had been married just three years.

Shortly after her death, staff began claiming they had seen Lady Louisa prowling the passageway where the incident had taken place, later to be called the 'Grey Lady's Walk.' Even today she is heard banging on doors in a desperate and endless search to locate the whereabouts of her footman. She was a beautiful young woman in life, and it is said by those who have seen her that she retains her beauty in death. The Grey Lady is the most frequently seen of Longleat's ghosts, even the Marquess of Bath claims to have seen her on occasion. Her portrait hangs in the Lower Dining Room.

After his wife's death, Thomas moved from Longleat to live in the village of Horningsham nearby. There were those who, at the time, spoke of his reasons for leaving; he lived in mortal dread of encountering Lady Louisa as she walked the passageway after nightfall.

Evidence to back up the death of the footman and subsequent ghost story are further endorsed when central heating was being installed in 1903. It had been necessary to lower the floors in the cellar to accommodate the boiler and pipes. Whilst digging up the flagstones, builders discovered the skeletal remains of a male wearing what appeared to be jackboots and fragments of a footman's uniform of the period. To avoid any scandal, the bones were collected and quietly interred in the local churchyard, only a few feet from where 2nd Viscount Thomas Thynne is buried.

The Red Library

Longleat has one of the largest private book collections in Europe. It has seven libraries containing some 40,000 books owned by the family since before the house was built. Nearly half of the eighty-five volumes which appear in the booklist of 1577 are still to be found on the shelves. One library in particular, the Red Library, contains 5,000 books and a rather distinguished ghost who is thought to be that of Thomas Ken, Bishop of Bath and Wells, who took refuge at Longleat when he lost his seat as punishment for refusing to switch his allegiance from King James to King William. He remained at Longleat for twenty years until his death in 1711 and his ghost has been seen sitting quietly in the Red Library reading, when approached he vanishes.

The Swan Omen

The legend of Longleat's swans dates from when the Thynne family occupied the house. Legend has it that should the swans ever leave Longleat then the family will be doomed. Visitors to Longleat will no doubt notice the vast number of swans that nest around the lake, as they have done for hundreds of years.

In 1916, the 5th Marchioness of Longleat noticed five swans flying low in formation and heading directly toward the house and the window she was looking out of. Fearing they would collide with the window she backed away. As she did so one swan broke formation and flew over the house, whilst the other four settled on the lake.

Swans flying in formation are not unusual but the Marchioness was well aware of the omen and worried something had happened to her eldest son, Viscount Weymouth who was fighting with his unit in France. The family rallied around her trying to dispel her fears. However, the following day she received a telegram informing her that her son had been killed in action just as she had feared.

Mompesson House and the Phantom Drummer of Tedworth

Mompesson House has been in the ownership of the National Trust since 1952. It is a fine example of Queen Anne architecture and stands prominently overlooking Choristers Green, Salisbury. It was built for Sir Thomas Mompesson in 1701 and completed by his son Charles, following his death. The house was constructed from Chilmark stone, the same stone used to build the beautiful cathedral opposite.

Was William Drury really responsible for the Mompesson House haunting and the legend of the Phantom Drummer of Tedworth? (© Christine Bozier)

Mompesson House is noted for its elaborate plasterwork ceilings, grand oak staircase, quality eighteenth-century furnishings and Turnbull glassware. Indeed, as you step through the carved stone doorway you would be forgiven if you felt you had been transported back to the early eighteenth century such is the decorative setting. The stunning plasterwork ceilings alone will captivated you as you search for nymphs, birds and mythological kings and satyrs. Film buffs amongst you may like to know that the scenes depicting Mrs Jennings' London home, for the British-American production of the 1995 movie *Sense and Sensibility* starring Kate Winslett, were filmed here. What many don't know about Mompesson House is its legend.

'The Phantom Drummer of Tedworth' (now Tidworth) was a report published by Joseph Glanvill in 1668 in his book *Saducismus Triumphatus* (*The Defeat of Sadducism*), which implies a denial of the afterlife and the teachings of Christ. Glanvill's investigation of John Mompesson and his family who resided in Tedworth was to become the stuff of legend; the Mompessons' were plagued by poltergeist activity between 1661 and 1663 following an encounter with a Mr William Drury.

In March of 1661, John Mompesson, a local landowner and magistrate learned of a disturbance whilst visiting Lugershall in Wiltshire. Apparently, a vagrant by the name of William Drury of Uffcott had become an intolerable nuisance in the high street by incessantly beating a military rhythm on his drum whilst marching up and down outside the local constabulary (immediately following the English Civil War many soldiers became licensed beggars with permits to beg their way home). It seemed Drury had an axe to grind, for he believed he was owed supportive recompense for his part in the Civil Wars where he held the post of drummer, a post of great responsibility. The Civil Wars claimed many casualties, none more so than drummers who were often on the frontline beating out commands via various drum rhythms. Drury persisted with his protest, producing a permit signed by magistrates of some note. The local constables were suspicious of the document and arrested Drury for causing an affray.

He was brought before the Justice of the Peace, presided over by John Mompesson and found guilty. His drum was confiscated. Mompesson had the drum sent to his private residence at Mompesson House until he had decided what to do with it. Drury spent the night in custody but the following morning made good his escape.

John Mompesson had been away in London when the drum arrived at his home. No sooner had the drum been delivered when all hell broke loose. When Mompesson returned he was greeted by his distraught wife, children and staff, all of whom had stories of mysterious knocking noises in the dead of night. When staff had gone to investigate the source of the knockings the sound would suddenly shift location. Sometimes they even seemed to emanate from within the very walls. The children complained of scratching noises coming from under their beds and of being lifted bodily from their beds by unseen hands. But worst of all was the incessant drumming. Many witnesses testified to the noises and especially the drumming which would beat out military rhythms at all hours of the day and night.

These disturbances persisted for over a year. There were frequent reports from family and staff of ghostly appearances, objects either being thrown about or going missing and of course the drumming. The noise was blamed initially on William Drury, who it was thought had managed to creep back into the neighbourhood with the sole intention of causing distress to the Mompessons. This theory was later dismissed for lack of evidence and, furthermore, Drury had been arrested for numerous other crimes and deported to the colonies (where he once again managed to escape). His freedom was cut short, for on his arrival back in England he was promptly arrested on the orders of John Mompesson. He was charged with the crime of evoking an evil spirit. Drury was found guilty and sent to Salisbury Gaol, where he was eventually released on appeal.

'These disturbances are typical of poltergeist infestations', concluded Joseph Glanvill, who was eager to publish his findings under the title of 'The Phantom Drummer of Tedworth'. Glanvill only managed to witness sounds of panting and scratching coming from the children's bedrooms. Of the drumming and other phenomena, he heard and saw nothing.

There was such a media interest in the case that King Charles II saw fit to send Lord Falmouth to investigate the furore.

With him came Lord Chesterfield, whom the queen instructed to make discreet enquiries. Neither envoy could find any explanation as to the source of the disturbances. A play was penned by Joseph Addison, the essayist in 1715 which became the stuff of popular folklore.

As a postscript, during the 1950s restoration work was being carried out inside the house. Denis Martineau, a former occupant of Mompesson House, received a visit from a Mr Hammick. During their meeting Hammick recalled the story of the ghost drummer, at which point Martineau excused himself and left the room. He returned only moments later with a brass drummer's badge from the English Civil Wars. It had been discovered under the floorboards of the room where the drum was said to have been kept under lock and key.

The phenomena petered out during 1663 but strange knocking noises still persist to this day, especially in the area of the library.

There is another version of this story with regards to the location of the Mompesson's residence. Some say the family were living at Zouch Manor (now a nineteenth-century farmhouse) in Tidworth, though some stories place them as living in one of the cottages close to the Norman church of the Holy Trinity, also in Tidworth. When I visited Mompesson House recently, the guides believed that the location of the legend resides firmly in Salisbury and who am I to argue?

The Haunting of Folly Wood

Folly Wood lies near the boundaries of Easterton and Eastcott. Here you will find a narrow farm track which cuts through an escarpment known for centuries as Maggot's Castle. The track slopes steeply down beneath the shadows of monstrous, ancient trees whose roots seem to have erupted from the crumbling greensand like weathered, gnarled fingers. I couldn't help but marvel at these towering giants which the elements have seen fit to lay bare. I wondered at the physics responsible for preventing them from crashing down into the valley below, such was their precarious grip of the sheer banks.

Folly Wood is so named because of a house that stood just north of the wood in the mid-eighteenth century at Maggot's Castle in Maggot's Wood (now Folly Wood). The house was originally called Castle House and was built by the wealthy Wroughton family of Urchfont around 1730. The Wroughton's were a prominent and respected family in Wiltshire; they owned Eastcott Manor and much of the surrounding lands.

It was in 1758 that Seymour Wroughton inherited the house, which he immediately set about modernising. He added six bedrooms, servants' quarters, garret, cellars, stables, gardens, three fishponds and an overly ostentatious gazebo which he placed high up on Maggot's Castle overlooking the valley below. Wroughton renamed the new house Maggot's Castle House. The construction of the gazebo, however, soon earned it the name Wroughton's Folly.

Seymour Wroughton was a recluse and a bit of a bad egg by all accounts, the black sheep of the family. Rumours began to circulate in the villages about girls who had ventured down to Maggot's Castle House and never returned. Suspicions grew that Wroughton must have had a hand in their disappearances, but no evidence was forthcoming so

The Haunting of Folly Wood. You would be wise not to venture here at twilight. (© Christine Bozier)

nothing was ever proved. The locals were so afraid of him that they refused to go near the place or accept offers of work there. Now the ghosts of young women are said to haunt Folly Wood at the site where the house once stood.

Wroughton died suddenly on New Year's Eve 1789 as a result, so it is said, from his excessive drinking habits. It was during one of his drunken outings that he met his fate on the farm track which leads down to the old drive and on to the house. Wroughton, worse for drink, was driving his coach and four in a reckless, wild manner when one of its wheels clipped a boulder and overturned, breaking his neck on impact. The horses in their panic struggled to free themselves from the confines of their harnesses. When they regained their feet they began dragging the remains of the shattered coach along the drive with Wroughton's lifeless body trapped and flopping about in a most grotesque manner like a rag doll. It is said that the boulder Seymour hit had been placed in his path purposely by the sister of one of the girls who went missing after visiting the house looking for work. Her revenge was sweet it seems. There is a wall plaque in honour of Seymour Wroughton at Urchfont Church, but there is no mention of how he met his demise, just his date of birth and death.

It is said, that should you venture down into Folly Wood at twilight on New Year's Eve you run the risk of encountering Wroughton's ghostly coach and four, and should you look directly into Wroughton's wild, staring eyes you should surely go mad. There have been stories of people hearing the sound of galloping horses close to where the house once stood. For many years following Wroughton's death, children were warned by their parents to be away from the wood before twilight, for if they stayed they would encounter 'Wild Seymour Wroughton'. I would have thought this warning enough to deter even the most defiant of children.

After Wroughton's death the house was auctioned. It was never lived in again and slowly fell into neglect, eventually becoming ruinous. The foundations were visible until the nineteenth century and the drive and a faint outline of the gazebo's foundations until the mid-1970s, but now they too have disappeared. The fishponds are still in evidence, though many trees obscure where the house once stood. It is rumoured that much of the building materials from the house went to build Potterne fire station.

There were many strange goings on linking to Wroughton's Folly in Folly Wood, as this newspaper report from January 1842 shows:

> Report of skeletons discovered at Stert (innkeeper named Burry at Lydeway allegedly murdered customers at the 'Shepherd and Dog'). A person said he knew a man who was a friend of Burry and heard him say that he had killed many a man between the Charlton Cat and Wedhampton and buried them at Wroughton's Folly.

Maggot's Castle House became known locally as 'Folly House' when it transpired it had been built on marshland and partly across one of the fishponds, a folly indeed. Shifting grounds, subsidence and the approximation of the fishponds to the house seem to have contributed to the eventual demise of the house.

Even today, many of the local villagers will not venture into Folly Wood as darkness descends. I did and I must say, ghost stories aside, at that time of day it is a pretty imposing place, make no mistake. I was effectively in the middle of nowhere; isolated and in a deathly quiet wood at a spot where the house once stood. It's very easy to see how some people get spooked.

Urchfont Manor

The village of Urchfont lies along the northern edge of Salisbury Plain, approximately 7 miles south of Devizes. Urchfont Manor dates from about 1680. It was built on the site of an earlier house from which a fireplace and some other fittings have survived and are now incorporated into the current building. It was Sir William Pynsent, who came to Urchfont village in 1678 and who was responsible for the construction of the new house.

Sir William Pynsent died in 1719 and the estate passed to his son and heir William Pynsent Jnr. On his death in 1765 he left the house (there was no heir) and its entire estate to the current Prime Minister, William Pitt the Elder. William Pitt later sold the property to the Duke of Queensberry, who already owned lands in the parish.

The manor had several owners before it was purchased in 1928 by Hamilton Rivers-Pollock. A distinguished lawyer, he lived there with his family until his untimely death in 1940. Hamilton Rivers-Pollock's life, it is said, was to be overshadowed by periods of depression possibly due to the crash of his fortune during the Second World War. It was on the 11 June 1940, during one of these desperate bouts of depression, that Hamilton

Urchfont Manor, home to a tragic history.

Rivers-Pollock gave all his staff the day off and took a loaded pistol. He approached his wife, who was seated at her piano, and shot her once through the head before turning the weapon on himself.

A column in a local newspaper of 11 June 1940 makes it clear that this was a very distressing case, as the couple were much respected in the community and a great deal of sympathy was felt for their children. Half the article talks about the couple's lives and their achievements and the second half goes into some detail concerning the inquest: 'Mrs RP was found with a bullet wound to the head and the conclusion was that suicide was not possible. Her husband, who had been in a distressed state, was found next to her and had shot himself through the mouth.'

The manor passed to Rivers-Pollock's son Martin, who leased the property in 1941 to London County Council. They converted it into a hospital for the care and convalescents of children evacuated from London suffering from tuberculosis. The manor was eventually bought in 1945 by Wiltshire County Council who established a residential centre for adult education. The college was officially opened in June 1947. Wiltshire County Council closed Urchfont Manor College on 3 October 2012 and it has since been purchased privately.

The ghost of a woman dressed in black, thought possibly to be Mrs Rivers-Pollock, is said to haunt the manor. One such encounter with the Lady in Black took place one Christmas several years ago. The staff had just finished locking the manor's many guest bedrooms in preparation for the Christmas holiday and had gathered in the dining room to enjoy a drink before going home. Suddenly, two members of staff noticed the figure of a woman passing the entrance to the dining room from the direction of the kitchen. Mystified and just a little concerned (bearing in mind that the manor was closed) they immediately went to investigate. Several minutes passed, when on their return they had to admit that there was nobody else in the building.

The kitchen is said to be haunted by a shadowy figure which is most often seen peripherally. Staff have been working at counter tops when they have been acutely aware of being watched.

Several years ago a course tutor staying overnight took a room in the main building. The following morning he described an eerie episode with regard to his duvet. He had woken in the dead of night feeling cold and noticed that his duvet was bunched up at the foot of his bed. Assuming he'd kicked it off in his sleep, he hauled the cover back over himself only for it to be pulled away moments later.

On a different occasion, a resident staying in the coach house (an outbuilding) questioned staff the following morning as to who might have been walking about in the dead of night and furthermore, who might want to rattle her bedroom door handle at that late hour.

Some of the housekeeping staff found servicing several of the top-floor bedrooms an uncomfortable experience, many claiming an intense feeling of being watched. Some years ago an electrician carrying out work in one of these rooms refused to work alone as he felt a presence was in the room with him.

The eighteenth-century Fiddlers Cottage situated in the grounds doubled as the village police station in the early 1900s. Before the college was sold it used to offer accommodation to course attendees. Some of the housekeeping staff would not work in this quaint little cottage unless the doors were left wide open, regardless of the weather; assumedly this was to allow for a quick getaway. Reports of footsteps padding across the ceiling above where they have been working when nobody but themselves have been in the cottage were not unusual, as was a strong feeling of something sitting on the stairs watching them.

Westwood Manor, Bradford on Avon

Set in beautiful, peaceful countryside, this fifteenth-century manor house has remained largely unchanged, other than a few alterations to its interior during the sixteenth and seventeenth centuries. The last owner of Westwood was Mr Edward Graham Lister, who was responsible for much of the twentieth-century restoration. Lister died tragically in 1953, following a motoring accident, and left the contents and endowment to the National Trust. Today the house is occupied by a tenant who administers it on behalf of the Trust.

It was a warm sunny afternoon the day my partner and I visited Westwood. What immediately struck us, as we stepped through the grey stone entrance into the grand hall, was that 'lived in' feel. This expression is used all too frequently for lesser properties, but in this case it is well deserved. Jacobean decorative ceilings (some dating from the late 1490s), grand Tudor fireplaces, oak panelled walls, Gothic oriel windows and not forgetting the handsome topiaried garden all added to that feeling of being welcomed.

Heavy, deep panelled oak doors led off to all the rooms. I had a vested interest in one in particular – the Corner Bedroom. It is said that if you manage to get a good night's sleep in this room you have done exceedingly well. For it is this room that is reputedly haunted by the ghost of a woman whose identity is a mystery.

Westwood Manor, Bradford on Avon, where a night's sleep in one of its bedrooms is fraught by disturbances.

Many guests who have slept in the Corner Bedroom have had eerie experiences and restless nights. Previous owner, Edward Graham Lister was in no doubt that the 'Corner Bedroom is most definitely haunted'. Many times he claimed to have seen the ghostly image of a woman or heard the lightest of footsteps emanating from that room. Guests and visitors alike have reported feelings of unease when spending any length of time in there. It is worth noting that the bed's elaborate, tapestried hangings were obtained from the famous haunted bedroom at Littlecote Manor near Hungerford. This was the scene, in 1575, of the heinous crime perpetrated by 'Wild Will' Darrell when he used his boot to hold his newborn son onto an open fire. That bedroom is said to be haunted by the mother of his child and the midwife who delivered it. Could this be a case of residual transference haunting I wonder?

I spent some time alone in the Corner Bedroom, just sitting there listening to a faintly discernible breeze as it sang mournfully in the eaves. My attention was drawn to the ornate stone fireplace, imagining what it would be like when a fire had been lit, I could almost hear the spit and pop from the knots in the firewood. I felt this would be a cosy room to spend a night in, but then I've not been disturbed by strange women in the dead of night (well not recently anyway!) I do recall a distinct stillness about the room; there was no movement to the air, as if time had stood still. There were few visitors that day so I pretty much had the place to myself, which may account for the stillness. I am reluctant to say the room is haunted but there was a definite feeling about it. My partner later remarked, when she had joined me, that she felt she could 'quite happily lose herself in here, such was its tranquillity'. I'm inclined to agree with her.

A former tenant by the name of Mr Denys Sutton claimed there was another ghost at Westwood. He said it was a distinctly unpleasant fellow that took the shape of a fearsome headless spectre and

/ander the house silently at night, he trousers off the unwary.

›f the guides recalled a story that the gardener had told her, a gentleman who has been in service at the manor for many years. He described having just entered the music room, when he smelt pipe tobacco and noticed it rising and curling above a high-backed club chair. The chair was facing away from him, so he could not see who was sitting there. He called out but there was no reply. He approached the chair but when he was but a few feet away the smoke instantly evaporated as if it had never been there. Gingerly he rounded the chair to face whoever was sitting there; you can imagine his surprise to find it unoccupied.

It is no secret that Westwood Manor is apparently cursed. The story goes that the manor was once the home of a magistrate who caught and sentenced a gypsy for poaching on his land. Hearing of her husband's arrest, his enraged wife marched up to the magistrate and vociferously cursed the house and family. Shortly after, the magistrate and his family started to have so much misfortune that they sold Westwood and left. The curse of Westwood Manor seems to have endured, for there have been reports of mysterious fires and violent deaths; one occupant supposedly hanged himself, another drowned and yet another threw himself from a second-floor window.

The manor has had many famous visitors over the centuries, such as Queen Mary who adored Westwood. She would often take a liking to a particular item of *objet d'art*, so much so that the household would have to discreetly hide objects that they thought might interest her on subsequent visits. This measure was taken so they would not be obliged to make yet another gift of her adorations. She was greatly loved by all at Westwood Manor. Her pen, the one she used to write letters with whilst staying there, is now in a glass box beneath her photograph in the Grand Hall.

Lydiard House

Lydiard House near Swindon was built in the seventeenth century and is a fine example of Palladian-style architecture. It was occupied for some 200 years by the St John lineage, pronounced sin-jin. Today the house is owned by Swindon Borough Council and used primarily as a conference centre. The council have done an admirable job in renovating the grounds and lake, and are to be commended for their efforts in making Lydiard House and park a pleasant visitor experience.

Probably the most famous of Lydiard's ghosts, is that of Sir John St John (1585–1648). His ghost has been spotted in the morning room and the adjoining library, where staff and visitors have reported seeing him leaning casually against the fireplace. A former caretaker by the name of Mrs Ingram said of the ghost, 'He appears quite solid, just like you or I and if it wasn't for his seventeenth-century clothes, then he would quite easily be mistaken for a living person.' Sir John's ghost is not confined to the house it would seem, for he has been seen several times strolling about the estate and sometimes approaching visitors where he will stand before them quite motionless before abruptly disappearing. His presence is frequently preceded by a strong sweet smell of tobacco and a sharp drop in temperature. His ghost has been described as morose and melancholy, not surprising given the tragedies he endured in life.

Lydiard House near Swindon, several ghosts haunt this splendid seventeenth-century mansion.

He was a staunch Royalist whose life had been marred by the tragic deaths of eight of his thirteen children born of his first wife. Three boys and a girl died in childhood, the eldest son Oliver predeceased his father and the three remaining sons, John, William and Edward died in the English Civil Wars. The latter is honoured by Sir John in St Mary's church, where a striking, life-sized, gilded statute of Edward emerging from a tent in full armour, holding a shield bearing the family coat of arms, stands magnificently in the south chapel. Sir John built the south chapel and installed his own tomb there in 1643 ahead of his death. It includes effigies of himself, both of his wives and his thirteen children. The detail in this alabaster, chalk and black limestone monument is exquisite and widely viewed as amongst the finest examples of its kind in England. His ghostly presence prevails to this day.

Other phantoms include the spectre of a woman dressed in white who has been seen several times on the staircase in the house. No one knows for sure who she is but some speculate she could be the ghost of Lady Blunt, whose apparition is said to appear every 30 October on the anniversary of her fiancé's murder. This story is not confirmed but the ghost certainly is.

The grounds are said to be haunted by the ghost of a Civil War drummer boy who has been seen silently tapping out a beat on a drum slung across his shoulder. A phantom coach and horses haunts the avenue that leads up to the house.

Lydiard House and grounds are open to the public but if you wish to visit the church, which is always locked, then you will have to obtain permission from the house reception.

2

CHURCHES AND ABBEYS

St Mary's Church, Lydiard Park

The church of St Mary's is situated in the grounds of Lydiard Park. It has its origins in the thirteenth century, though the church you see today is largely fifteenth century. It is reputedly haunted by the ghost of a grey, cowled figure and many who have witnessed the apparition report a strong feeling of malevolence. There have been several members of

St Mary's Church, Lydiard, a malevolent presence lurks within.

staff who, in the past, have refused point-blank to enter the church alone after experiencing intense feelings of being watched. There have been incidences of people being chased out of the church and through the graveyard, followed by the sound of heavy footsteps. People have also reported hearing organ music emanating from within the church after it has been locked and secured. Other phenomena include the sound of a weeping woman and flitting shadows in human form, though only ever perceived peripherally. I must say that despite being full of beautiful objects, the church does exude a certain atmosphere.

St James Church, Avebury

The church of St James stands on an early Saxon stone church and to the west of Avebury's Neolithic stone circle. The Saxons were a suspicious bunch and believed the sarsen stones to be possessed by malevolent spirits, so built a church just outside the henge to counter evil's nastiest. Fourteenth-century Christians took this belief one step further and toppled the giant sarsens into pits where they were buried in the hope that doing so would deconsecrate what they saw as a pagan temple.

The original church dated from around AD 1000 but has since undergone many alterations over the centuries, mostly by the Normans who added several features, one of which is an elaborately carved, arched doorway to the south. The tower was added much later, built in the fifteenth century. At its base stands an early twelfth-century Norman font, with carvings that show two serpents with twisted heads facing the figure of a bishop holding a crosier. This was an image popularised in the

St James Church, Avebury, where a chance encounter with a ghostly little boy may have proved fortuitous for one couple.

Middle Ages, depicting Christ trampling on the dragons of evil and sin.

Sightings of a mysterious female figure in the churchyard have been reported many times. When approached she will turn and look in your direction before fading to nothing. Could these sightings be linked to the discovery of a female skeleton found in the churchyard during the mid-1950s? Her remains were exposed whilst a fresh grave was being prepared to receive the recently departed. The skeleton was identified as being in her early 20s and was surrounded by shards of late Norman pottery. She was lying east to west within the churchyard boundary and it appeared to represent a Christian burial of the Norman period. Maybe disrupting her grave triggered her ghostly presence.

The Little Boy in the Churchyard

Another frequently spotted ghost in St James churchyard is that of a little boy dressed in Victorian clothing. One particular story is charming and has an unexpected and rather delightful outcome.

The story goes that a local woman and her 2-year-old daughter had just popped down to Avebury village to post some letters. On returning home, they decided to take a shortcut through the churchyard. It was mid-morning on a clear day in March as they passed through the lychgate and into the churchyard. Going down the pathway towards the church, her daughter suddenly pointed at the church door from her pushchair. Her mother stopped and looked in the direction she was pointing and saw a little boy of about 8 years old hopping up and down on one of the table tombs by the church door. She later described him as 'solid in appearance and dressed in a short brown jacket with matching knickerbockers cropped at the knees where they met with white stockings. He wore a brown cap, from which poked out a tousled mass of mousy brown curly hair that framed the cutest of rosy-cheeks.'

Intrigued by his appearance and thinking he was part of some local play or the like, they approached him. He paid them no heed as they covered the short distance, absorbed in his game of tomb-hopping. They were little more than a few yards away when he looked up in mid-hop, smiled, then abruptly vanished into thin air.

The unexpected outcome to this story is that soon after her encounter with the little boy the woman fell pregnant, which was a wonderful surprise to her and her husband as she was judged infertile after the birth of her daughter due to ovarian cysts. She still lives locally and has a lovely little boy who she adores. Coincidence, or something a little stranger?

St John the Baptist and St Helen Church, Wroughton

The village of Wroughton lies 3 miles to the south of Swindon. Earliest evidence of a settlement here can be traced back to the Mesolithic, although archaeology for that period is a little thin on the ground. Many scattered finds unearthed throughout the area indicate a settlement at Wroughton during the Neolithic, not surprising when you consider its close proximity to the Avebury complex.

The Grade I listed church of St John the Baptist and St Helen was built of dressed sarsen stone. The original church, of which nothing remains, first appeared in the Ellendune charter of AD 956 appending the recognition of a boundary wall.

St John the Baptist and St Helen Church, Wroughton, where a Victorian premature burial may have caused the Ash Lady haunting.

The construction of the current church began in the twelfth century. What can be seen today is mainly fourteenth century and in the case of the tower, fifteenth century. More recent restoration work was carried out in the nineteenth century by T.H. Wyatt in 1846. Further work was undertaken in the 1850s, 1880s and in 1905.

The Haunted Yew

When I visited St John's and entered the churchyard I was immediately drawn to the immense yew tree to the south, its canopy covering some 50ft or so. Centuries-old headstones encrusted with lichen stand in its shadows, their inscriptions long since eroded by the passage of time. As I approached the tree a sudden gust of wind disturbed its branches, causing its heavy bulk to creak and groan like an old sailing ship. It was at that moment I was reminded of the stories surrounding this grand old fellow.

I had lived in Wroughton for most of my childhood and had heard the stories about the haunted tree in the churchyard. Tales of folk encountering the ghostly figure of a man believed by some to have hung himself from its very branches earned it a place in local legend. Many people have described a chilling feeling of 'being watched' as they tend to the graves of loved ones. Others claimed to have had a fleeting glimpse, a peripheral sighting if you like, of a 'shadowy figure' standing close to, or under the tree. Sightings of this mysterious wraith still occur today. The figure is always described as wearing black, his features indiscernible and concealed by the deep shadows cast by the tree.

There is folklore attached to this grand old giant which, as kids, none of us ever had the courage to try out. The tale goes that should you run around the tree anticlockwise thirteen times on the stroke of midnight you will

The Haunted Yew Tree, the location of the mysterious man in black.

summon the 'Tree Ghost'. What is not clear however, is what method should be deployed to send the tree ghost back from whence it came once it was summoned. If I recall, the ambiguity of the tale's outcome was enough to deter us kids from playing out the ritual, not that we would have been allowed out anyway.

The Ash Lady

Many Victorians lived in dread of vivisepulture (premature burial) as their understanding of coma, catalepsy and disorders of the nervous system were in their infancy. Their fear arose at a time when burial sites in England were at a premium; it was common to dig up old graves and store the bones in 'bone houses' allowing more space for the recently deceased to be 'planted'. It would be a gruesome discovery when exhuming the dead to find evidence of a struggle to break free, which was unfortunately the case for 1 in 25 of those buried at this time.

For those who could afford it, many Victorians went to extraordinary lengths to ensure they would not fall victim to a living entombment. The thought of being pronounced dead and then waking up in the suffocating blackness of one's own coffin was just too much to contemplate. One example of countering taphephobia (a fear of being buried alive) was to instruct the undertakers (before one's death of course) to make a small hole in the lid of the coffin where a chain or piece of rope would be passed through and attached to the corpse's wrist, whilst the other end was affixed on top of the filled grave to a post with a bell attached to it. I can't help but wonder who would be prepared to sit all day and all night beside a grave, just in case its occupant should wake and tinkle the bell. It was this bizarre practice that gave rise to the expressions 'saved by the bell', 'dead ringer' and 'the graveyard shift'.

It was not until 1852, when the stethoscope became widely available, that there was a noticeable decline in errors regarding the pronouncement of death.

It is widely rumoured, though not confirmed, that a young woman was buried alive at St John the Baptist during the early nineteenth century. Shortly after her burial, it was discovered to the horror of the family physician that the woman was subject to seizures which would paralyse her entire body, giving the impression of death. Her coffin was hastily exhumed and when opened it was clear to all that the body had moved since burial. To their horror they discovered deep scratches on the underside of the coffin lid, made as the terrified woman desperately tried to claw her way to freedom.

Could the ghostly figure of a woman wearing a tattered, ash-coloured dress in the style of the Victorian period be that of the poor wretch who met her death as a result of premature burial. She is most often encountered at the north end of the churchyard where she stands quite motionless until approached, whereupon she will fix you with an icy stare before vanishing.

Malmesbury Abbey

In the year 1010, a young monk by the name of Elmer resided at Malmesbury Abbey. Now Elmer had a burning ambition to fly like a bird, in fact the pursuit of manned flight occupied much of his free time. As a young man he had read of the fabled flight of Daedalus and his son Icarus on waxen wings to Sicily. This gave him an idea, he would set about designing a set of wings to carry him skyward.

After much work perfecting (or so he thought) and assembling a set of wings, he climbed to the top of one of the abbey's towers, possibly the Saxon watchtower which is no longer there. With a curious crowd gathering below, he attached the wings to his arms and feet. He then climbed onto a ledge, said a short prayer and dived off.

Malmesbury Abbey, where a monk silently searches amongst the headstones.

Elmer managed, so it is documented, to glide a distance of some 200m before gravity took over and the Flying Monk of Malmesbury came down with a thump, breaking both of his legs. This would have put most people off but Elmer was undeterred and during his lengthy recuperation it was discovered that he was making plans for a second flight, which he announced would include much-improved aerodynamics to his wings and the addition of a tail flight. News of his plans reached the bishop, who immediately forbade Elmer from taking part in any more flights of fancy from the abbey towers, or anywhere else for that matter.

For many years (he lived till he was 88) Elmer would hobble about Malmesbury dreaming of flying once more. Alas it was not to be. He did, however, gain much notoriety as a distinguished scholar for his research into manned flight. His winged image can be seen inside the abbey rendered in stained glass.

Could the ghostly figure of a hooded monk, which has been seen many times amongst the headstones in the abbey grounds, be that of Elmer? The figure is said to move silently amongst the headstones as if searching for something, then suddenly raise its arms heavenward in a eureka gesture as if that certain something had been discovered. Maybe Elmer is looking skyward at a passing aircraft and thinking 'we did it in the end!'

Lacock Abbey

Lacock abbey was founded in 1232 by Ela, Countess of Salisbury, the first Abbess of Lacock. She came from a rich and powerful family, inheriting her father's title when she was just 6 years old, and became a ward of King Richard the Lionheart. She was later to marry William Longspree, the king's illegitimate brother. Lacock Abbey was built in his memory.

Canonesses (nuns) occupied Lacock Abbey from 1232–1539. There would have been at least fifteen women at any one time living at the abbey. They would have led a frugal life; each day would be spent in almost total silence, rising at 2 a.m. to take part in one of seven religious services. They would have had no contact with friends and family, devoting their entire lives in the service and worship of God.

Following the Dissolution of the Monasteries (1536–1541) by King Henry VIII, the Lacock estate was put up for sale and purchased by Sir William Sharington (1495–1553) treasurer of the Bristol Mint. He kept the magnificent thirteenth-century cloisters (used in the Harry Potter movies) and the fifteenth-century chapter house, but decided to add an impressive mansion. It is this building which is reputedly haunted by a hideously deformed dwarf who appears dressed entirely in black. It is said that many years ago two children were staying at the house when they saw an 'ugly little man' walk through their room. Several years after this encounter the skeletal remains of a deformed dwarf were found buried in the wall of that particular room. The identity of this unpleasant little fellow remains a mystery and his spontaneous appearances have caused those who encounter him to flee in terror.

A little ornate lake in the grounds is said to be haunted by the ghost of a beautiful young woman dressed in a white gown, which appears to float

Lacock Abbey, haunted by a hideous dwarf.

behind her as if caught by a gentle ethereal breeze. She is most often seen strolling beside the lake and her expression is 'mournful' or 'melancholy'. It is thought this beauty may be the ghost of Rosamund Clifford, often called 'The Fair Rosamund' or the 'Rose of the World', mistress to King Henry II who was besotted with her at a time when he had lost favour with his wife Queen Eleanor of Aquitaine. Clifford's death in 1176 was both untimely and mysterious, for it was rumoured that she had been killed on the command of a jealous Eleanor, though these accusations were never proved. Just why it should be Clifford that haunts the lake is unknown, other than it may have been a favourite haunt of hers, no pun intended.

Lacock is probably best-known for one of its former resident families, The Talbots, who succeeded the Sharingtons. Years later one family member, William Fox Talbot (1800–1877), who was born and died at the abbey, was to receive wide acclaim for his pioneering work in the field of photographic negative development. A museum dedicated to his work occupies part of the abbey. One of his first surviving photographs was taken at the abbey in 1835. It shows a grainy picture of one of the abbey's oriel windows taken near the west steps using one of his tiny rudimentary box cameras.

Many years later, a photographer taking pictures at the west steps had a very strange encounter. He was framing a shot when he noticed a beautiful young woman standing close to the steps looking up at the abbey. He made sure the figure was in the centre of his viewfinder and took just one photograph of her, as he was eager to make the young lady's acquaintance. He started to walk towards her but when he was only a

The west steps at Lacock Abbey.

few yards away she abruptly disappeared. Stunned, he immediately made enquires in the abbey as to who he had just seen. He was surprised to find that he was not alone in witnessing the young lady, for many similar sightings had been reported at the foot of the west steps. Later, when the photographer was developing the film, he was surprised to find that although the picture of the west steps was perfectly framed, the mysterious young lady was not evident on the negative. It is thought that this ghost may also be that of Rosamund Clifford.

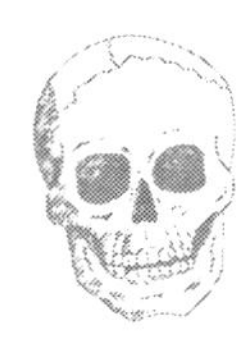

3

BARROWS AND HILLS

The Devil's Den, Clatford Bottom

The Devil's Den dolmen stands alone in a field at Clatford Bottom on Fyfield Down near Marlborough. The word dolmen is believed to be a derivative of the word Dillion, meaning boundary mound.

The Devil's Den, is a Neolithic burial chamber which was first recorded in 1723 by antiquarian William Stukeley. His illustrations show a long barrow of considerable length with several large sarsen stones which have all but disappeared now, no doubt victims of agriculture. Today the structure

The Devil's Den dolmen, Chatford Bottom, haunt of the demon dog.

comprises of just three massive sarsens and a capstone arranged similarly to that of a Welsh 'Cromlech.'

The structure was rescued from imminent collapse in 1921 by archaeologist A.D. Passmore. Restoration work was undertaken to shore up the dolmen by incorporating a concrete support to one side engraved with the year of its salvation – 1921.

The late Guy Underwood dowsed the site in 1958 following up the work of Reginald Smith, an authority on the Neolithic age. After his survey was completed, Underwood concluded that the megalith was built over a 'geospiral'. Those interested in earth energies and ley lines will know what a geospiral is, but for everyone else (me included) it means a 'blind spring' which is said to generate a powerful surface spiral. Any the wiser? Me neither. Underwood believed the Devil's Den has one of the most powerful geospirals in the country and it may have been chosen by the dolmen builders for that reason.

Ancient tombs and tumuli seem to court folklore. There are tales of a ghostly sentinel dog with burning red eyes which is said to lie in wait beneath the mound, possibly guarding the spirit of its long-dead master. The eerie baying of a hound has been heard echoing across the valley in the dead of night. Spectral dogs are not uncommon at burial mounds and their roots can be traced back to Celtic mythology.

Another tale involves the Devil himself, who is said to yoke up four white oxen at the stroke of midnight in an attempt to dislodge the capstone. Just why the Devil should want to do this is unclear. On top of the capstone are several dimples or 'cups'. The tale goes that should you fill these dimples with water then overnight the water will mysteriously vanish, apparently consumed by the fiend that haunts the dolmen.

How to get there:
Because it's easily missed by road, I have included what I hope are directions that even I could follow. From Beckhampton roundabout, take the A4 to Marlborough. Just before you enter the town, there is a left turn marked Manton House and The Hollow; it's easily missed, so keep a sharp eye out for it. Follow the lane till you arrive at the car park, some 2 miles or so. From the car park, bear right onto a track and you will see the dolmen in the valley to your left after about 5 minutes of walking.

The White Cat on the Ridgeway

The Ridgeway is a 5,000-year-old pathway which was used by drovers, traders and probably invaders as they traversed the Wiltshire Downs. These travellers would have clung to the safer, upper slopes of the hills, for the lowlands were covered by thick forest and swamp which would have been impassable and treacherous in places.

Today, the 89-mile stretch covers Wiltshire, Berkshire and the Chilterns. It snakes through Wiltshire's prehistoric landscape, passing hill forts, ancient sites, dolmens and countless tumuli, all of which add colour to the Ridgeway's legend, myth and magic. It can also be wild and spooky at times. Amongst the many strange tales associated with this ancient pathway there is one in particular that has frightened many a traveller: the Ridgeway's fearsome 'white cat'.

A fiendish white cat is said to stalk walkers on the ancient Ridgeway passage. (© Christine Bozier)

The cat is reputed to follow walkers for miles whilst always keeping its distance. Some have described the encounter as being 'unnerving', almost as if the animal was 'stalking' them and the cat has been described as 'dirty-white', 'dishevelled', 'mangy' and about the size of a 'small dog'. When approached, the cat becomes unusually hostile, adopting an aggressive stance whilst hissing and spitting.

An encounter with this mysterious cat happened to a good friend of mine several years ago; I shall call him Philip. I never get tired of hearing Philip's story (it's his party piece), maybe it's the varied inflections in his tone that builds the tension and suspense. He tells a good yarn does our Phil, though I am inclined to consider this particular story genuine.

It was mid-August and it had been a sweltering hot day, the kind of day when all you want to do is stand in the doorway of WHSmith and bathe in their glorious air conditioning. Philip had previously arranged to meet with some friends that evening at a pub close to Avebury with the intention of camping out under the stars.

They duly met as arranged and enjoyed a meal and a few drinks at the appointed pub before eventually setting off towards the hills and the campsite Philip had earmarked as a good spot. It was also decided that it would be rather fun to go mushroom picking along the Ridgeway at first light, no doubt to compliment the breakfast to come.

Sure enough the following morning, as the dawn chased away the night's shadows, they packed up their gear and set out across the mist-shrouded hills. They hadn't gone far when one of the party noticed they were being tailed by a particularly large, mangy white cat. They stopped to take a closer look at the wretched creature, not easy considering it was partially obscured by the dawn mist. One of the female members of Philip's party attempted to encourage the animal to come a little closer, but it would have none of it and seemed content to keep its distance, some 30m away or so. They decided to walk on but as they did, so the cat would follow them, when they stopped, so too would the cat. This went on for a mile or so until they came upon a Bronze Age round barrow. To their surprise as they began to climb the barrow the cat, which until now had been tailing them, suddenly appeared on top of the barrow directly in front of them. The party stopped dead in their tracks as the creature arched its back, raised its hackles and hissed and spat at them. Quite how it had managed to pass them and leap onto the barrow without them noticing was later cause for much debate.

The party were startled not just by the animal's sudden aggressive behaviour, but by the way it reacted when they tried to climb a little further onto the barrow. For any advancement was immediately met by more hostility. Philip and his party, now a little wary of kitty, nervously backed away from the menacing-looking animal, at which point the cat seemed to become a little less aggressive, although it continued to emit an ominous mewing. The slightest attempt to approach the barrow was instantly thwarted by more displays of belligerence.

It was decided to leave the animal well alone, so the party slowly headed off in the other direction, turning frequently to check on the cat; none were keen to discover the animal had taken to following them again. The cat remained on top of the barrow until line of sight was eventually obscured by a hill.

The cat's behaviour was perplexing. Some of Philip's friends thought the animal just plain bonkers, whilst others, including Philip, were a little less hasty to dismiss the cat's strange behaviour. Philip, to this day, believes that the cat was warning them to stay off the barrow for reasons unknown.

Spirit animals, usually dogs but occasionally cats, are thought to guard barrows and dolmens. I wonder if Philip and his friends encountered such a creature on that misty August morning, as they walked the ancient hills of Wiltshire's Ridgeway in search of mushroom delights?

Adam's Grave

One of my favourite spots in Wiltshire (I have many) has to be the impressive group of hills that stretch between the villages of All Cannings and Alton Priors. Within this group stands Wiltshire's highest point, a point that has given rise to many light-hearted debates over the years amongst the locals. It was claimed by some that Tan Hill at All Cannings was the highest point, whilst others disputed this and countered that nearby Milk Hill at Alton Priors should carry the title of 'king of the hills'. To settle this debate, a survey was carried out in 2009 by a team from the BBC's *Countryfile* programme using state-of-the-art satellite GPS technology. Accompanying the BBC was Paul Denyer from Ordnance Survey using similar equipment. Their combined findings proved that Milk Hill at 294.19m just pipped Tan Hill to the post at 293.93m, a mere 26cm separating the two. Both stand at around a 1,000ft above sea level and offer splendid views across the Vale of Pewsey and Salisbury Plain.

These beautiful rolling hills are part of the ancient Ridgeway passage, walked by shepherds, drovers and tradesmen for thousands of years. Strange tales of spooky encounters have been handed down over the years, not just by shepherds and the like but more recently by hill-walkers. One spot in particular has attracted more than its fair share of strange tales: a trapezoidal long barrow called Adam's Grave, one of Wiltshire's most spectacular long barrows.

Adam's Grave (or Woden's Burg to use its Saxon name) is set high up on Walkers Hill between Milk Hill and Knapp Hill. Its position is certainly meant to be noticed. The Neolithic barrow is approximately 60m long by 6m high and is flanked either side by two deep ditches approximately 6m wide by 0.9m deep. At the south-east end there are two sarsen stones known as 'Old Adam' and 'Little Eve' which mark what would have been the entrance to the barrow (it is no longer open). The burial chambers show evidence of oolitic limestone drywall construction similar to those at West Kennet Long Barrow 4km to the north, close to

Adam's Grave. A giant is said to slumber here.

Silbury Hill. The barrow was opened in 1860 by John Thurman, a noted local archaeologist, but was probably pillaged earlier by 'hill diggers' looking for treasure. Four incomplete skeletons were discovered and removed along with a leaf-shaped arrowhead, indicative of Neolithic flint working. The barrow is a dramatic construction that would most likely have been the final resting place of some dignitary.

Adam's Grave was thought to be the final resting place of a giant. According to legend, if you run around it seven times you risk waking him and suffering his wrath. Just the thought of having to run around this huge tumulus seven times is enough for me to ensure the giant's continued slumber.

In her book *Ghosts and Legends of the Wiltshire Countryside* the late Kathleen Wiltshire, who spent some forty years collecting stories of local folklore in Wiltshire, recounts a story told to her by a Miss Murial Cobern:

> Miss Cobern had an experience on Walker's Hill in the summer of 1965 or '66. She was walking back from the barrow above the White Horse, towards the lay-by at the top of the hill, where she had left the car. About fifty yards from the barrow she suddenly felt very uneasy, and glanced around; it was very cloudy and rather cold, and no one else was about. A flock of sheep through which she was passing seemed untroubled, so she went on. Suddenly she could distinctly hear horses' hooves thudding, as if a whole army was coming at full gallop; but there was not a horse to be seen anywhere. Miss Cobern, walking much faster she admits, passed Adams Grave, and could hear the hooves no longer.

I wonder whether Miss Cobern may have inadvertently been privy to a ghostly re-enactment of one of two battles that took place near to Adam's Grave, both of which are recorded in the *Anglo-Saxon Chronicle*.

The first battle was fought at Woden's Burg in AD 592. The *Chronicle* states, 'Her micel wælfill wæs æt Woddes beorge, 7 Ceawlin wæs ut adrifen.' (There was great slaughter at Woden's Hill, and Ceawlin was driven out.) Ceawlin was king of Anglo-Saxon Wessex. In most versions of the *Anglo-Saxon Chronicle* the entry does not record the identity of the force opposing Ceawlin, though it is thought they were most likely British.

The second battle in AD 715 records the entry: 'Her Ine 7 Ceolred fuhton æt Woddes beorge.' (There Ine and Ceolred fought at Woden's Hill.) Ine was king of Anglo-Saxon Wessex and Ceolred was king of Anglo-Saxon Mercia. The identity of the opposing force is not recorded.

The topography of the area would have been of strategic importance to the Saxons and a prize worthy of conflict, since it lay close to the passage of Wansdyke where the ancient Ridgeway interconnects. The passage was known by the name of 'read geat' (red gate) or 'gap' (passage) by the Saxons and it is likely they defended Woden's Burg on many occasions.

It is known for horses to give flight for no apparent reason in the hills near Adam's Grave and along the Ridgeway towards Knapp Hill, and galloping hooves where there are no horses can also be heard. Tales of eerie encounters with ghostly figures abound, as do reports from folk who have heard the chilling howls of baying hounds (thought to be barrow guardians) echoing across the misty hills at dawn.

Standing on top of Adam's Grave and gazing down on the dramatic, ancient landscape prompts thoughts of the fearsome battles that have taken place here, of the agonising cry of men cut down and the snort and whinny of terrified horses. Battlefields have long been associated with hauntings, so it is conceivable that the horrific conflicts which took place during those battles would have etched an 'imprint' or 'residue' into this now tranquil landscape.

Avebury Stone Circle

The construction dates of the Neolithic henge and stone circles at Avebury are estimate at between 3000–2400 BC. The monument, a designated World Heritage site, is the largest of its kind in the world and attracts some 500,000 visitors annually. Many of the massive sarsen stones (an immensely hard, silicified quartzite sandstone formed around 23 million years ago) that make up the three circles within the 'henge' (a banked ditch, often encircling a ring of standing stones or wooden posts) would have likely been close at hand, lying on top or partially buried within the chalk landscape. Others would have been sourced from the Marlborough Downs and dragged on wooden rollers (logs) or sledges greased with animal fat, an impressive feat considering some of them weigh around 100 tonnes. In preparation for erecting the stones, pits were dug and wooden stakes driven into the ground to prevent them from overbalancing. The stones would then have been hoisted into position using leather straps, fashioned rope, wooden levers and a massive amount of manpower. Once upright, the stone's base was packed with more stakes, chalk rubble and smaller sarsen stones until it was securely in position. The close proximity and abundance of stones must have been a deciding factor when the 'stone builders' were looking for somewhere to erect their monument. The whole project is estimated to have taken 1.5 million man-hours, using only the most rudimentary of tools: antler picks, ox scapulars and flint axes.

The Avebury stones. Hugging one is not recommended.

Just what motivated our ancestors to build such an elaborate structure largely remains a mystery. In the absence of any written records, generations of archaeologists have had to piece together the monument's history through recovered fragments. Some have theorised that it was a place for sacrificial offerings, and it's true that animal bones have been discovered, along with knives, flints tools and pottery; these finds may have played a part in rituals to appease the gods, ensuring a good crop yield and the continued fertility of people and animals. The banked ditch may have served as a public theatre, an elevated platform for the faithful to gather and observed the rituals taking place within the circles.

Some favour the astral observatory theory and believe the stones were placed in some sort of geometrical plan. Those in the north-east quadrant or Cove, along with a third stone (now destroyed with many others during the seventeenth and eighteenth centuries), were thought to align with the moon's northern-most moonrise. If true, this may have been to pay homage to the Neolithic moon goddess. This theory is difficult to prove as many of the stones are missing, making any alignment with the moon and stars speculative at best.

It is possible that the monument was erected to 'commemorate' the dead. If this theory is true, then the monument would have been a sacred place where the transition of the dead from this life to the next would have been venerated.

Folklore has evolved over hundreds of years regarding the alleged power of Avebury's sarsens. These enigmatic giants appear to cast a spell on many who see them. Some believe the stones have healing properties and so hugging one will release its magical properties and cure ills; people have claimed to feel vibrations emanating from within a stone's very core whilst hugging it. 'Stone hugging' is a common sight at Avebury. When I pass through I can pretty much guarantee that somebody will be flat against a stone, adopting a pose reminiscent of the crucifixion whilst gazing heavenward in eager anticipation of the legendary 'vibe'. Alternatively, the vibe might well be attributed to the rumble of heavy traffic passing close by on the A4361. In the fourteenth century many Christians believe the stones were harbingers of ill luck, which suggests hugging one is probably not such a good idea. For this reason they toppled many stones into pits and buried them.

With all the magic, mystery and ancient rituals that have grown up around the stones, you would have thought them a supernatural hotspot. If truth be known, the opposite is pretty much the case, especially when compared to the generous helpings of ghostly activity from the likes of The Red Lion pub (the only pub in the world to stand inside a Neolithic stone circle), the stately Tudor Manor and twelfth-century churchyard of St James, not forgetting reports of ghostly hitchhikers on the A4361 and the famous coach and four said to thunder through the village at night. The few hauntings that have been reported from the stones are as follows …

Back in the 1960s a woman driving through the village late at night reported seeing ghostly figures dressed in period costumes, dancing amongst the stones. I would suspect that what she actually saw was nothing more than one of the many pagan rituals and parties which take place at Avebury.

There are claims of dwarf-like creatures seen darting amongst the stones in the dead of night, and of a spectrum of tiny twinkling lights believed by some to be fairy folk. These lights have been seen countless times dancing above the stones, especially the mysterious Diamond Stone or Swindon Stone, which is located at the north-west quadrant. This stone is said to uproot itself and cross the A4361 at the stroke of midnight, no mean feat at around 50 tonnes.

Continuing the twinkling light theme, the henge is supposed to be a hotspot for UFO activity. Many sightings have been reported of strange airborne anomalies which are said to buzz the stones. Then there are the elaborate, mysterious crop circles that seem to conveniently appear close to the monument around the summer solstice, why should that be I wonder?

In the south-east quadrant you will find the massive Devil's Chair stone. Here, many have sat to have their photograph taken but I do wonder how many would stick around if they knew that the 'chimney' (the top of the stone) is said to belch black smoke as a warning that the devil himself is in residence. There is a legend that if you run around the stone anticlockwise 100 times you will evoke the devil. These stories were probably put about by pagans to prevent zealous Christians from attacking and burying the stones. Sadly it didn't work.

Some claim that the henge was constructed on top of several ley lines (veins of invisible energy beneath the earth, said to connect ancient megalithic sites, monuments and buildings, particularly churches). Dowsers especially believe the lines intersect beneath the henge and so are most likely responsible for generating subterranean earth energy, which may account for some of Avebury's strange goings on.

There have been reports of poltergeist activity in some of the cottages in the village which were built from sarsen stones ransacked from the henge. A friend of mine, who several years ago rented what is now 'The Lodge', was convinced the place was haunted. Many items, especially in the kitchen, would go missing only to mysteriously reappear days later. He lived alone incidentally.

Avebury is a fascinating place and well worth a visit, if only to marvel at its construction and debate its mysteries. That said, the claims surrounding the stones abilities will, I'm sure, stretch even the most vivid of imaginations.

The Battle of Roundway Down, Devizes

It is no secret that Wiltshire's downland once ran red with the blood of many a battle-slain soldier. If it wasn't Mercian against Saxon, then it was Parliamentarian against Royalist. One such battle took place on Roundway Down near the town of Devizes during the English Civil War.

Following the stand-off at Lansdowne Hill near the town of Chippenham a few days earlier, Sir William Waller, commander of the Parliamentarian army was eager to engage the Royalists at the soonest opportunity. He decided to lay siege to the town of Devizes, where he was told the Royalist, Lord Ralph Hopton (who had been injured during the Lansdowne encounter) had taken refuge. Waller, seizing the opportunity to have another pop at Hopton, gave the order to advance on Devizes. Unfortunately for Waller, Hopton had

Looking into Bloody Ditch from Roundway Down.

already sent word detailing his predicament. When Waller reached Devizes he was horrified to find the superior forces of the Royalists cavalry and foot soldiers, commanded by Sir John Byron and Lord Wilmot, waiting for him. A fierce battle ensued at Roundway Down, 1 mile north of Devizes, on the 13 July 1643.

As the battle raged, Waller could only watch in horror and disbelief as his men were cut down. Finally, in a desperate bid to escape the carnage, the Parliamentarians fled to nearby Roundway Hill where they were cornered by the Royalists' Cavalry. A deep and dramatic escarpment fell away to their rear (the foot of which is now aptly named 'Bloody Ditch') which claimed many lives that day, and not just those of the Parliamentarians. The Royalist cavalry, having been given the order to charge, inadvertently followed the fleeing Parliamentarians over the abyss to their deaths; men and horses broke their necks in the steep fall.

Over 4,000 men engaged in battle on that day and in excess of 600 of those perished at Bloody Ditch. Some were buried nearby at Rowde and Devizes on the 14 July and some have been discovered in shallow graves on Roundway Down. These individuals had been stripped, their skeletal remains showing evidence of sabre and bullet wounds. The whereabouts of the remaining soldiers is a bit of a mystery but many scholars speculate, because of the logistics in moving so many men and horses, that they were likely buried where they fell at Bloody Ditch.

What had started as a favourable stronghold for Sir William Waller's Parliamentarians ended in a crushing defeat, a defeat that would go down in history as one of the most decisive Royalist victories of the English Civil War.

The bodies of the fallen Parliamentarians were stripped and pillaged by the Royalists, however some items are still being recovered. Artillery artefacts, often unearthed by local farmers, have included cannon balls and discharged carbine shot.

Standing atop Roundway Down and looking down into Bloody Ditch still sends an icy chill down my spine. It can be a desolate and windswept place at the best of times, often shrouded in a swirling mist and it is not surprising to find it has a very haunted history. Reports still abound of ghostly musket and canon fire echoing across the valley. Sounds of horses in distress and the terrified screams and shouts of long-dead soldiers are still common to this day. Though spectral horses have been seen plunging to their deaths over the escarpment, there have been few sightings of actual soldiers. The Down is well known for its eerie mists that swirl along the valley floor and drift down from the top of the escarpment. It is from these mists that the majority of ghostly encounters are witnessed.

Roundway Down and Bloody Ditch are now nature reserves where many species of wild flowers and insects can be found and if you're lucky you may just spot a deer or two.

How to get there:

From Devizes on the A361, turn into Folly Road by the Travelodge Hotel. Follow the road out of Devizes into Roundway village and from there follow the road uphill till you reach a fork. Then take the right fork, you will see a white chalk horse carved into the hill on your right. Follow the road till it forks again and take the left fork. At the top of the hill follow the gravel track for about a 0.25 mile till you reach a car park, you are now on Roundway Down. Access to Bloody Ditch and Roundway Hill are through the gate just off the car park to the left, marked 'Nature Reserve'.

Silbury Hill

Silbury Hill stands just off the A4 between Beckhampton and Marlborough and is the largest prehistoric man-made mound in Europe. It is estimated to have taken some 4 million man-hours to build. Those who started it never saw it finished, nor did they envisage how much it would have developed upon its final completion. To this day its true purpose remains largely an enigma.

Radiocarbon dating from the last conservation/excavation in 2007–2008 by English Heritage has confirmed that work started on Silbury around 2400 BC, give or take a generation, which puts it on the cusp of the Stone Age and Bronze Age. The conservation work by English Heritage and civil engineering company Shanka to 'shore up' Silbury after the summit imploded in 2000 as a result of years of indiscriminate tunnelling by treasure hunters, gave archaeologists one last chance to excavate the monument before English Heritage sealed it for good in 2008.

Silbury measures 150m (492ft) in diameter, 36m (120ft) in height and 30m (98ft) across its summit. It was built in three phases and is thought by archaeologists to have taken around 400 years to complete. In other words, someone didn't wake up one day and announce it would be a jolly good idea to build a 120ft-high chalk hill in one hit. Silbury was constructed from clay, turves, gravel, flint, sarsen stone, chalk and 'worked' chalk. When finished it would have stood out; a gleaming white chalk beacon in the landscape for all to see.

Silbury's prominence in the landscape and its close proximity to other ancient monuments (such as Avebury,

Enigmatic Silbury Hill.

Windmill Hill, The Sanctuary and West Kennet Long Barrow) would suggest it may have been used for religious ceremony. Unlike Stonehenge, there is no evidence to suggest Silbury had any astronomical alignment. Neither was it ever intended as a fortification, although at some point during the Saxon occupation the summit was levelled to allow the construction of a defensive building.

More fanciful theories for Silbury's construction have grown over the centuries, here are just a few:

1. A burial site for King Sil or Zel, whose golden effigy was thought to sit astride a fabulous golden horse which sparked a frenzy of treasure hunters over the centuries. King Sil's ghost is said to ride around the foot of Silbury when the moon is full.

2. A solar observatory, or giant sun dial, which may have been used to measure the seasons. Silbury does cast a shadow north towards Avebury.

3. A huge fertility symbol dedicated to the earth goddess. This would have been very important to primitive farming communities at a time when life depended on the continued growth of crops and livestock.

4. There is a tale involving the devil, who, on his way to bury the town of Marlborough under a sack of earth (folklore is a bit vague as to why the devil had it in for Marlborough) encountered the priests of Avebury. A heated argument ensued, whereby the devil was forced to drop his sack of earth where he stood and hey presto! Silbury was born. Lucky old Marlborough if you ask me.

5. 'Fairy Hills' from Irish folklore. Fairies, elementals and nature spirits were believed to inhabit ancient man-made mounds, just like Silbury. But a warning for the unwary who blindly venture onto the hill enticed by the muffled sounds of revelry and gaiety

emanating from within the mound; all is not what it seems. Although you will be welcomed and promptly invited in to eat, drink and be merry by these ethereal entities, your eventual return to the real world will leave you horrified, for at this point fairy folklore becomes a little darker. As you were innocently partying within the mound, 100 years have elapsed and all those you love and cherish are long since dead.

6. A preparation for a landing stage for aliens spaceships, because Silbury looks a little like a flying saucer! Some believe the builders of Silbury were first visited by aliens who showed them how to build it. It is true that Silbury has been a hotspot for UFO sightings in the past.

Ghostly Roman soldiers are also said to walk close to Silbury's base. Recent geophysics carried out by English Heritage discovered a small Roman settlement just south of Silbury close to the old London road, the A4.

Standing before Silbury Hill, one can't help but marvel at what is quite simply a staggering feat of engineering. You may consider, as I have done, what drove prehistoric man to undertake such a project. Silbury was most definitely constructed for a purpose but we will probably never know precisely what. It remains a stupendous enigma, a masterpiece of human ingenuity and creative genius.

Please note: Silbury Hill is privately owned and access to the hill is strictly forbidden. This is to help prevent any more erosion and damage inflicted by thousands of visitors over the years.

West Kennet Long Barrow

The West Kennet Long Barrow is situated on a ridge opposite Silbury Hill about a quarter mile off the A4 between Beckhampton and Marlborough and about 1.2 miles from Avebury. It dates back to around 3700–3600 BC, predating Silbury Hill and Avebury.

The barrow is 104m (341ft) long by 2.4m (8ft) high, making it one of the longest barrows of its kind in Britain. It was originally flanked on three sides by a ditch approximately 3m (10ft) deep by 6m (20ft) wide. Dug from solid chalk, this impressive mound would have, on completion, stood out stark white on the hillside. At some point a semi-circular forecourt was added to the entrance which faces east/west, an alignment that at first light would catch the rising sun and illuminate the barrows interior. Around 2500–2200 BC, for reasons unknown, the tomb was filled with chalk and soil and its entrance sealed with giant sarsen stones. This would seem a final gesture, a transformation, possibly from one belief to another. The sealing of the tomb was also at a time when work had started erecting the stones at Avebury.

The barrow was under threat from hill diggers (opportunists searching for treasure and the like) from as early as the seventeenth century. One such hill digger was a Dr Troope of Marlborough, who plundered the barrow to retrieve human bones which he ground up to make his 'noble medicine that relieved my distressed neighbours'. I am not surprised that his neighbours were 'distressed', especially if they happened to discover the ingredients of Dr Troope's medication, or maybe they already knew. His indiscriminate digging

West Kennet Long Barrow, possibly the oldest haunting in England.

consequently damaged several sections of the barrow which thankfully have since been restored.

In 1859 John Thurman, a local archaeologist, was granted permission by the land owner to excavate the site with the understanding that no sarsen be disturbed. As a result Thurman entered the barrow from the top, where he located and cleared the far western chamber. Here he discovered six incomplete human skeletons, one of which was an infant. Other discoveries included pottery and worked flint. However, Thurman stopped at the one chamber and missed out on the golden egg.

It was much later, in the mid-1950s, that Stuart Piggott and Richard Atkinson cleared four chambers that Thurman had missed. In so doing they discovered the scattered remains of another forty-six individuals, both adult and infant. Examination of the bones identified many of the occupants as long-term sufferers of severe arthritis, spina bifida, twisted limbs and polydactyl (extra digits to hands and feet). Some remains showed bone fractures, probably as a result of a brawl or fall. Abscesses and impacted wisdom teeth were also discovered, but few cavities. It is thought the children may have succumbed to influenza or pneumonia; such diseases leave no trace on bone, as was the case here. One individual was of particular interest. An adult male, he was found in the left chamber as you enter the tomb, fully articulated and squatting in a corner with a leaf arrowhead embedded in his neck. It was a hard life back then, where you were lucky to reach 35.

What you see today, following Piggott and Atkinson's restoration, are the five burial chambers set laterally either side of a 10m corridor with the largest chamber situated at the far western end. The interior is of sarsen stone corbelled with huge sarsen capstones. One stone in particular is extremely smooth to the touch. This stone is a *polissoir* or polisher stone, used to sharpen stone axes. What is unusual about this stone is that it stands upright, as polissoir stones were always used horizontally so water could be used as a lubricant during the sharpening process. This means that the polissoir stone is much older than the barrow itself and was placed there when it had become superfluous. Only about a sixth of the barrow has been excavated and the remainder awaits further examination.

Long barrows were foremost places of burial but also focal points for rituals. Rituals are still enacted today amongst followers of earth religions. There is also evidence of occult rituals but the two bear no relation. Many see barrows as a door to another world, a liminal, a place of intense spiritual awareness. The remains of offerings are frequently found within and fruit, flowers, corn, candles and incense serve as a reminder of how important the barrow is to some.

The barrow, which is now part of the Neolithic Avebury complex, is one of the most visited and best-preserved burial mounds in Britain. It may also claim to have one of the oldest hauntings in the country, possibly the world.

One Man and His Dog

It is said that at dawn on the longest day, the figure of a man dressed in white robes, possibly the ghost of one of those buried within the tomb, has been seen standing on top of the mound accompanied by a large powerful hound with red ears. The pair stand silently and quite motionless at the barrow's eastern end, presumably waiting for sunrise. At first light, they turn in unison and enter the tomb below. Several local farmers, whose profession ensures an early start, have witnessing this strange eerie spectacle.

There have been occasions where people reported intense feelings of dread when inside the tomb. Some even claim to have seen figures moving therein and the faint sound of whispered voices.

Early one morning in 1992, a holidaying couple had a terrifying experience whilst inside the barrow – well one of them did, the other was actually outside during her ordeal. She had been exploring the interior, when all of sudden she was grabbed by unseen hands which attempted to pull her towards the deepest part of the chamber. Later, when she emerged from the barrow in a state of shock and her partner had helped her to regain some composure, she told him of the terror that had taken hold of her and how desperately she had fought to free herself from the invisible clutches which held her fast. She described how her whole body had become inexplicably 'weighed down', like she was walking through deep mud, making any movement a huge effort. It transpired she had only been in the chamber minutes but the whole sorry episode felt to her like an eternity.

4

INNS AND PUBS

The Cross Guns Inn, Avoncliff

Atop a steep valley in the picturesque hamlet of Avoncliff, stands the Cross Guns inn. Built in 1496 as a private residence, it is one of Avoncliff's oldest buildings. The terraced gardens offer a splendid view of the Avoncliff triple-arched aqueduct, designed and built by John Reenie and John Thomas between 1797 and 1801. It carries the Kennet and Avon canal over the River Avon and Box Railway. This impressive stone-built edifice ranks as one of the most magnificent of Britain's waterways constructions. The Cross Guns inn is situated just 100 yards from Brunel's original wide-gauge railway, which must have served the hungry and thirsty railway workers during its construction.

The house became an inn in the early 1600s, taking the name The Carpenter's Arms. As the years passed alterations were inevitable. First the east was changed to accommodate the many millworkers, quarrymen and travellers. The west was updated when the canal arrived in the early part of the eighteenth century, to accommodate the influx of rail workers, working boatmen (bargees) and their horses, which would have been stabled behind the old cellar block.

In 1794 the 9th Battalion of the Wiltshire Rifle Volunteers was formed and duly established a rifle range beside the inn. It was decided to honour the local yeomanry by changing the inn's name to the Cross Guns. The inn was purchased in 1999 by current owners Ken and Jenny Roberts and remains a family run free house.

The Blue Lady

At a time when there were no roads to speak of in Avoncliff, folk would often use a footpath which led down from the top of the valley, passing behind the inn and down to the river below. It just so happens that the old footpath would

The Cross Guns inn, Avoncliff. Is this the most haunted inn in Wiltshire?

have passed directly through what is now the ladies' toilets, which is where the Blue Lady is most often encountered.

Of all the phantoms reputed to haunt the Cross Guns, the Blue Lady is the most frequently seen. When encountered she is always dressed in blue or blue-grey in the style of the Victorian period. She is occasionally sighted in one or two rooms within the inn and the gardens. Anglers fishing on the banks of the Avon and boaters who have moored on the canal have reported fleeting glimpses of her as they make their ascent from the valley floor en route to the inn. She is said to stand quite motionless looking down at the river from the gardens. You can imagine the look of shock when visitors reach the inn only to be told by staff that the Victorian lady dressed in blue you have just described is probably one of our ghosts.

One of the first sightings of the Blue Lady was by a member of staff named Janet, now sadly deceased, and her encounter took place about ten years ago. She had just popped outside to the ladies', when moments later the inn's door burst open and in came Janet in a state of panic claiming she had just seen a woman step out of the wall in the ladies' toilet.

Now it is unclear if there were people in the inn at the time but if there were, I can only imagine it must have caused quite a stir. Another member of staff, Christine, eventually managed to calm Janet down long enough for her to relate what had happened. Janet stumbled nervously through her story; she described how she had been heading for the exit of the toilet when all of a sudden a woman stepped out of the wall blocking her way. Terrified, but managing to muster courage from heaven-knows-where, she made a dash for the door which meant having to pass directly through the apparition, which she did.

The woman was dressed in blue-grey with wild staring eyes. Janet also recalled the woman's ankle-length boots which, as she raced for the inn's door, were heard 'click-clacking' behind her as if the Blue Lady were in hot pursuit. She did not turn round to confirm if she was being chased, and who could blame her?

Janet claimed to have seen the Blue Lady several times since that night, but nothing was quite as traumatic as her first encounter. She was not the only person to encounter the ghost; over the years several customers have come racing back into the inn as white as sheets with similar stories. Some witnesses, a little more curious than terrified, return with friends no doubt hoping to get a second look. They never do.

The Blue Lady's arrival is often preceded by a noticeable drop in temperature, an element that seems to figure in many ghostly encounters, and many staff and visitors have felt an icy chill moments before she manifests. Such an incident occurred one evening while a party were having a meal beside the cosy, inglenook fireplace in the lounge. A female member of the party suddenly complained of feeling intensely cold and looked about to see if a door had been left open. At that very moment, she saw quite plainly a woman in grey-blue glide partway through the lounge and into the public bar. She was the only one in the party to have witnessed the apparition.

I spent some time chatting with the landlord, Ken Roberts, who also recalled an incident. One sunny afternoon, two women were sat in the garden having a drink when, for no reason other than feeling 'watched', they glanced up at a first floor window (used in the 1500s as a family room). Here they saw an elderly woman smiling back at them, wearing what appeared to be a white bonnet. They watched in utter amazement as the figure slowly disappeared before their eyes. This description does not seem to fit that of the Blue Lady but then there's more than one ghost haunting the Cross Guns …

Ken admitted to only ever having one ghostly experience and even now he is not totally convinced it was supernatural. He and a friend had been waiting patiently for the bars to empty as they were working on a new website for the inn and Ken's friend wanted to take some cosy atmospheric photographs of the interior with nobody in it.

Shortly after the last customer had left, in the lounge there suddenly appeared 'two strange lingering lights which seemed to hover above our heads'. At first Ken thought it was smoke from the log fire, or possibly a reflection caught by the light from somewhere. These explanations were quickly dismissed when the lights started to move about the room. Ken's friend took several photographs in quick succession and the results Ken says, 'have been interpreted differently by all who have seen them.'

Ken has never seen the Blue Lady or any of the other ghosts reputed to haunt the Cross Guns. He has always felt that with so many reports of strange goings-on, it would be foolhardy to refute anything that his staff and customers have seen.

One of several photographs taken that night. (Kind permission of Roger Jones)

Many of the inn's ghosts have been observed peripherally, as a fleeting image from the corner of the eye. Tall shadows resembling human form are a frequent occurrence in the kitchen. The chef, Robert, claims to have seen a portly woman resembling a Victorian housekeeper standing in the doorway to the kitchen, not once but on several occasions. One such sighting was shared by his colleague Christine, who was sitting in an adjoining room when she saw the same apparition via a mirror on the wall. The housekeeper disappeared as quickly as she had appeared. Robert and Christine looked at one another and asked, 'Did you see that?' in unison. They both had, as it turned out.

Another ghost is that of an elderly gentleman thought to be an eighteenth-century bargee, who is occasionally seen seated on one of the settles in the public bar. Christine claimed to have seen him one late night as they were closing. At first she assumed he was a customer who had been chatting to Ken, so thought little of it until she mentioned it moments later to another member of staff. Her colleague looked surprised and told Christine that she must be mistaken, as she had just come from that area and Ken was quite alone. But there was no way the gentleman could have left through the front door without Christine seeing him. Immediately she returned to the bar to find that Ken was indeed alone, washing glasses. She asked him if he had seen the old gentleman but he had not; it seemed on this occasion, Christine had been privy to yet another of the Cross Guns' resident ghosts.

Staff laying tables in the lounge in preparation for the evening diners have spoken of seeing a hooded figure resembling a monk standing by the inglenook fireplace, or on occasion disappearing into, or standing close to the cellar door. The cellar is said to have a tunnel which leads down to the river, though investigations have not been undertaken to confirm this. Several steps down from the lounge there is a little anteroom which hides a priest hole. Diners here have claimed to feel 'uncomfortably nervous'.

Several years before Ken bought the inn, the ghostly disturbances were so frequent that the previous landlord had called on the Dean of Salisbury to bless the inn. A blessing took place but alas, with little or no effect; some of the staff at the time firmly believed it even accelerated the phenomena.

So, is the Cross Guns the most haunted pub in Wiltshire? Well it certainly has a remarkably history of ghostly encounters, encounters I may add that are still being reported to this day. I think it would be naïve of me, or anybody else for that matter, to dismiss all the accounts as figments of the imagination, a trick of the light or some other well-intended explanation. I am sure that there's something in the Cross Guns, but just what that something is will remain open to debate.

Should you wish to stay at the Cross Guns inn then accommodation can be arranged. Many ghost hunters have spent eventful nights here, some, according to Ken, with interesting results. One group of researchers from Swindon stayed overnight and claimed to have witnessed several small children playing on the aqueduct in the dead of night, a most curious practice given the hour.

The Cross Guns inn is a cosy little place offering excellent locally brewed beers by Box Steam Ales, which incidentally is also owned by Ken Roberts and family. I can recommend the 'Tunnel Vision' but not if you're driving, or walking for that matter. A traditional menu of home-cooked food awaits the weary traveller and you never know, the unexplained too. Oh and ladies, do take care in the loos, you never know what you might bump into.

The Sign of the Angel Inn, Lacock

This fifteenth-century inn, formerly a wool merchant's house, is a fine example of a traditional English pub: oak beams, log fires, polished wood floors and antique furniture add to its cosy

Note the inclusion of a 'resident ghost' mentioned on the pub notice board.

The Sign of the Angel inn.

'lived in' appeal. The name, The Sign of the Angel derives from the 'gold angel' coin that was in circulation at the time of the pub's opening.

The inn is said to be haunted by the ghost of an elderly woman who has been seen frequently over the past twenty years or so. She is believed to be one of the previous landladies who simply refuses to leave. A friendly soul by all accounts, she has been spotted several times by staff and diners patiently sitting at one of the tables in the lounge bar. She also frequents one or two of the guest bedrooms. She is friendly spirit to some maybe, but not to a certain carpet-fitter who, in 1980 whilst laying stair carpet, experienced the ghost first-hand as she appeared right in front of him. He left the premises in somewhat of a rush vowing never to return.

I was amused to read the inn's notice-board and its reference to a 'resident ghost'.

The Haunch of Venison, Salisbury

The beautiful cathedral city of Salisbury lies to the south-east of Wiltshire on the edge of Salisbury Plain. Salisbury's origins can be traced back to around 3000 BC when an Iron Age hill fort (Old Sarum) was constructed about 2 miles north of where the modern city now stands. When the Romans invaded, they established a garrison and small market town here and named the hill fort Sorviodunum, a precursor to Salisbury.

Over the centuries the Romans, Normans and Saxons have all left their mark. When the Romans left, the Saxons used the site as a fort to ward off marauding Vikings. The Normans took advantage of the fort's strategic position and built a motte and bailey castle which was later replaced by a stone keep in 1100 and a royal palace in 1130.

Haunch of Venison, Salisbury, haunted by a cheating card sharp.

Old Sarum was the site of the first of Salisbury's cathedrals, built in 1092. Unfortunately it burnt down just five days after it was consecrated. A new cathedral was built around 1190 which caused tensions between the castle guards and the clerics, often resulting in violent clashes. The church became so exasperated by these frequent conflicts that in 1219 Bishop Richard Poore wrote to the pope, expressing his concerns and asking permission to build another cathedral well away from the current one. His request was soon granted, and a new cathedral was built at a location, so it is said, decided by an archer's arrow. 'Wherever the arrow should land will be the spot where the new cathedral shall be built,' instructed Poore. By chance the arrow landed most fortuitously on lands already owned by the church. A settlement soon grew around the new cathedral and eventually developed into the Salisbury of today.

The town has many fascinating and beautiful old buildings but one in particular, the Haunch of Venison in Minster Street, must rate as one of its quaintest. The tiny little pub was built in 1320 and is certainly one of Salisbury's oldest hostelries, if not one of its oldest buildings. In the 1300s it was often frequented by craftsmen who were working on the new cathedral's spire. It was also a place of ill repute (by today's standards that is) for the pub's cellar housed a brothel and secret tunnel which led to the local church; a popular passage for those not wishing their identities to be compromised.

As you enter the pub and step to your right you will find yourself in the 'Horsebox' bar, if you can get in that is, for this bar has to be the smallest of its kind that I have ever visited. The main bar to the left of the entrance is considerably larger. It has a beaten, pewter bar top, believed to be the only one of its kind in England, and a set of gravity-fed antique taps dispensing spirits and liquor, along with traditional hand pumps. Above the small bar are huge timber ceiling beams, many such beams were often salvaged from ships so it is likely that these too have a nautical provenance. The ancient oak wall panels are complimented by sturdy oak benches. It has a black and white tiled floor, said to have come from the cathedral, and an open fire which bears the date of the Spanish Armada (1588) adds a touch of cosiness to the surroundings. It is said that Churchill and Eisenhower once used this bar to plan the D-Day landings, a meeting not so difficult to believe when you consider Salisbury's long history of military installations. It is likely then that the citizens of Salisbury were all too familiar with the top brass moving within their midst.

The Haunch of Venison is said to be Salisbury's most haunted pub. Probably the most famous of its ghosts (there are two) is that of the Demented Whist Player, whose identity in this rather gruesome tale is not recorded. The story goes that sometime during the 1820s a stranger passing through town en route to Southampton arrived looking for lodgings. He happened on the Haunch of Venison which at that time was renowned as an 'English Chop House' – a place of fine eating. When this particular evening was over that title would take on a more macabre association.

The pub was full of regulars eating, drinking, playing games and generally making merry when the stranger entered the pub. The room fell silent, a little like one of those old spaghetti westerns starring Clint Eastwood. Unperturbed by the icy reception, the stranger walked to the bar and ordered a tankard of ale, which he then downed in one. He replaced the tankard back on the bar, turned to face the locals then tossed the pot boy a single gold coin demanding, 'ale for all!' This show of hospitality eased the tension in the room and the stranger was soon asked to join a card game, which he accepted. As the game progressed the stranger's luck seemed to grow and he won hand after hand. The room once again fell silent as the locals' attention was drawn to the stranger's uncanny run of luck. He won enough to pay for his lodgings for the night plus cover his ale costs several times over. One of the card players, a butcher who had been sitting close to the stranger and had become increasingly suspicious, suddenly produced a blade and with the swiftest of motions chopped off the stranger's right hand. As the stranger screamed in agony and dashed from the pub holding his bloody stump the other players looked to the floor where the hand lay. Grasped in its grisly grip were *five* bloodied aces.

During renovations about 100 years ago, a mummified hand holding nineteenth-century playing cards was discovered walled up behind a fireplace in the House of Lords bar upstairs. The find was thought to be that of the cheating card player, so it was placed in a locked display cabinet and attached to the wall, no doubt a deterrent to any would-be thieves. In March 2004 the hand mysteriously went missing, stolen from its case. News of the theft was carried by the media around the world. Strangely, it was reported that it had mysteriously reappeared back in its case some six weeks later, none the worse for wear. However, having spoken to the landlady I discovered that the hand was never actually returned and the exhibit upstairs is an accurate replica.

The pub is said to be haunted by the ghost of the vengeful card player. Many who visit complain of suddenly feeling icy cold in some parts of the building and staff often hear doors slamming when nobody is about. Lights are mysteriously switched on and off, dirty glasses are moved about the bar and items go missing only to reappear weeks later. Many of these strange events are often accompanied by the musty smell of freshly turned earth and wet leaves.

Another ghost said to frequent the Haunch of Venison is that of a woman in a white shawl. The story goes that about 100 years ago she sent her son on an errand to the pub to purchase a few bottles of ale. He never returned. Whether he was robbed and murdered for the few pennies he had with him, met with an accident, or simply went missing was never confirmed. To this day her distraught spectre has been seen inside the pub and immediately outside the building, where it is said she still searches for her missing son. Some of the regulars claim to feel her presence in the main bar. The figure of a woman in a shawl has also been seen ascending the stairs which lead up to the restaurant.

The Red Lion, Avebury

The Red Lion started life as a seventeenth-century farmhouse until it was granted a license to serve ale in 1802. Over the years it has gained a reputation for being one of the most haunted hostelries in Britain. It is unique for being the only public house in the world to stand at the centre of a huge Neolithic ring of standing stones.

There have been many reports of ghostly goings on at The Red Lion, including a horse-drawn carriage which has been heard to draw up on the cobblestones immediately outside the pub. This ghostly apparition is said to start its journey from the original south gate of a sixteenth-century manor house in the village. Those who have witnessed it tell of a huge black horse harnessed to a carriage without a coachman, emerging from a swirling mist as it thunders through the village before pulling up outside the pub where it disappears in a flash of lightning.

In the restaurant, staff have noticed some rather unpleasant odours akin to rotting eggs. The lights in the bar have a habit of spontaneously switching on and off, the CD player will occasionally start up at full volume and cutlery has been known to mysteriously rearranged itself after tables have been laid. There are even stories of a ghostly waiter who never asks for your order but instead stands motionless at your table until spoken to, at which point he abruptly disappears.

Upstairs there are two reputedly haunted bedrooms. One is the Private Bedroom, where several guests have asked to be moved to another room. When asked why, they have responded by claiming the room makes them feel 'uneasy'. The Private Bedroom has three ghosts: a woman called Beth, who stands gazing out of the window and two children who have be seen holding hands and cowering in a corner as if threatened.

The second of the two haunted bedrooms is the Avenue Room, which has two adult ghosts, one male and one female. These two have an unpleasant habit of popping up beside the bed, or rising up through the bed, doubtless

The Red Lion at Avebury, the only pub in the world to stand in the centre of a mysterious prehistoric stone circle.

a residue from a time when no bed was on that spot. There have also been occasions where guests have had to fight to keep their bedclothes from being pulled off by unseen hands in the dead of night. Other witnesses to this phenomenon have just watched in abject horror as said bedclothes are ripped from them and thrown to the floor. Some have checked out the same night vowing never to return.

A landlord is said to have been murdered here in the early eighteenth century by a band of outlaws who forced him to keep them hidden in the cellar to avoid detection by the authorities. He complied with their demands but unfortunately for him, had obviously seen and heard far too much for the gang to allow him to live and so they stabbed him to death. The spectre of what is thought to be the dead landlord now haunts the cellar and by all accounts he is a pretty fearsome sight. Drenched in blood and brandishing a knife (not too sure why it should be he who is brandishing the knife) he has caused horrified staff to flee the cellar in fear of their lives.

The Lady in Black

Probably the most famous of The Red Lion's ghosts is Flori. In the restaurant, there is a table set close to a large bay window, above which hangs a chandelier which has been seen to swing from side to side of its own accord. This is believed to be a sign that Flori (a young lady from the seventeenth century) is in close proximity.

Those who claim to have seen her described her as solid in appearance, in her early 20s with shoulder-length hair and dressed in a long dark skirt, matching bodice and puffed sleeves at the wrists. Flori is said to have perished at the hands of her jealous husband who had returned home unexpectedly from serving in the English Civil Wars. Eager to surprise her, he crept into the farmhouse and up the narrow stairs. When he reached their bedroom door he heard muffled voices coming from within. Gently lifting the latch he stepped into the bedroom only to discover Flori in the arms of another man. A scuffle broke out between the two men, whereupon her lover fled leaving Flori to her fate. Consumed with rage, her husband put his hands about her throat and squeezed the life out of her. He then carried her corpse down the stairs and out into the night where he dispatched her body down a well.

The story does not end there though. As the weeks and months rolled by, inquisitive village folk grew more and more suspicious of Flori's absence. Awkward questions were mounting, questions aimed at Flori's husband, enquiring as to her whereabouts, questions that became more difficult to answer. The truth became more difficult to conceal. Eventually, filled with guilt and remorse, Flori's husband confessed to his crimes and was later found guilty and hanged.

Flori ghost is most frequently sighted in the ladies' toilets (most inconvenient) and on occasion standing close to the well, or gliding across the upper floors from room to room. It is said that you have a better chance of encountering Flori if you have a beard. Apparently she is not too keen on men with facial hair and will set the chandelier swaying in the restaurant immediately above the table where a bearded gentleman is seated.

An investigation was launched by a team of divers in the early 1990s to try and establish if any human remains could be found at the bottom of the well. Although a thorough search was undertaken, nothing was ever found. It is fair to point out that the investigation was hampered by several large boulders which obscured the very bottom of the well. The investigation was deemed inconclusive and the whereabouts of Flori's body remains a mystery. Could her remains lie beneath the boulders I wonder?

The well has become a focal point, now situated inside the pub in the aptly named Well Room. The top is covered with tempered glass and the 86ft shaft is bathed in an eerie green glow.

The Waggon and Horses, Beckhampton

Just off the A4 between Marlborough and Devizes stands a quintessential English pub named The Waggon and Horses. Built in 1669 primarily as a coaching inn, it was originally named The Black Bear and was mainly constructed from sarsen stone. This would have been found locally in abundance, either on the Marlborough Downs or possibly Avebury, at a time when Neolithic stone circles offered little interest other than for building material; examples of which are in the construction of several of the cottages in Avebury village. In 1724 The Black Bear was renamed to The Hare and Hounds, possibly in response to the hare coursing which was prevalent in the area at that time. Finally in 1823 The Hare and Hounds became The Waggon and Horses. This name no doubt derived from the waggoners and drovers who frequented the inn having travelled long and hard on what is now the A4, a popular route used to drive livestock between Bath and London markets. The inn offered accommodation, grazing land for cattle, a stable and a smithy.

Today the pub's close proximity to Silbury Hill, the chambered tomb of

The Waggon and Horses, Beckhampton, featured in Dickens' Pickwick Papers.

the West Kennet Long Barrow, Avebury Stone Circle and the medieval market town of Devizes make for an ideal watering hole. It is just what's needed after a day exploring the mysteries of Wiltshire's ancient landscape.

The Waggon and Horses has a claim to fame as it appears in Charles Dickens' *The Pickwick Papers*. It is very likely that Dickens visited the inn at some point during his travels to Bath, a city he is said to have loathed, describing it as 'a mouldy old roosting place, built by a cemetery full of dead people'. What follows is an extract from the *The Pickwick Papers*, describing what is believed to be Tom Smart's visit to the inn:

> Tom cast a hasty glance at the upper part of the house as he threw the reins to the hostler, and stuck the whip in the box. It was a strange old place, built of a kind of shingle, inlaid, as it were, with cross-beams, with gabled-topped windows projecting completely over the pathway, and a low door with a dark porch, and a couple of steep steps leading down into the house, instead of the modern fashion of half a dozen shallow ones leading up to it. It was a comfortable-looking place though, for there was a strong cheerful light in the bar-window, which shed a bright ray across the road, and even lighted up the hedge on the other side; and there was a red flickering light in the opposite window, one moment but faintly discernible, and the next gleaming strongly through the drawn curtains, which intimated that a rousing fire was blazing within. Marking these little evidences with the eye of an experienced traveller, Tom dismounted with as much agility as his half-frozen limbs would permit, and entered the house.

Two ghosts are said to frequent the area of the public bar. Locals and staff have been startled to find an elderly lady dressed in what appears to be a white smock standing at the customers' side of the bar. Some who have seen her think she might be the ghost of a previous landlady. Her features are described as 'unclear' or 'misty', so no positive identification has ever really been forthcoming. She is quite harmless and when spotted will immediately vanish.

The second ghost is an elderly gentleman dressed in the style of the Victorian era. He has been seen leaning against the fireplace whilst smoking a pipe and is accompanied by a small dog which is curled up at his feet. Sometimes the unmistakable aroma of pipe tobacco has been noticed near the fireplace.

The A4, which passes immediately outside the pub, is said to be haunted by a coach and four; hooves and the clatter of carriage wheels have been heard to draw up on the cobbled forecourt. The local police have said in the past, that the thunderous, audible distraction to passing motorists is believed to have been the cause of several accidents on the approach to the Beckhampton roundabout.

The old Roman road that passes close to Beckhampton was once a notorious spot for highwaymen who would seize every opportunity to rob the wealthy as they journeyed by coach from London to Bath in the seventeenth and eighteenth centuries. This 'rouges thoroughfare' may also account for several other reports of ghostly coaches and horses seen hereabouts and also the occasional sighting of a caped figure wearing a tricorn hat, believed to be the ghost of Walter Leader.

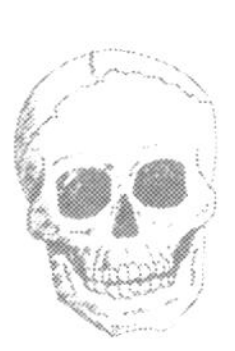

5

HOTELS

The Black Swan Hotel, Devizes

The medieval market town of Devizes has gained quite a reputation for its plethora of hauntings. It would appear the town has more spooks per square mile than just about anywhere else in Wiltshire. Wherever you go you are never far away from a ghostly tale or two and many of the town's pubs and houses are haunted, as are several of its roads and pathways.

The Black Swan Hotel in Market Square was formerly a private residence until 1737 when it became a coaching inn. The Black Swan stands opposite where the town gallows once stood. The current function room used to serve as a court of judgement and Masonic meeting place for the towns dignitaries in the 1700s. I'm sure many a soul was placed on trial and found guilty within the confines of that room, and how convenient it must have been to have the gallows so close by.

The late fifteenth-century cellars beneath the hotel predate the current building. They go back to a time when the site was occupied by the Nags Head inn and consist of five chambers leading off from the centre structure; one of these chambers appears to have been deliberately bricked up. Local historian and author of several books on Devizes subterranean tunnels, John Girvan, sought permission to carefully remove several bricks and in so doing discovered what he believes to be a labyrinth of secret tunnels which run under Market Square, possibly connecting with other buildings including Devizes Castle. It is within the main cellar that one Ambrose Saintsbury is thought to have kept his horse and a change of clothing, and he may well have used the tunnels for his nocturnal transgressions.

The Black Swan Hotel, Devizes, where you may get more than you bargained for if you book room 4.

The Publican Highwayman

Ambrose Saintsbury was one of several proprietors of the inn during the 1700s. It was alleged that he led a double life, as a respected publican and pillar of the community by day and a ruthless highwayman by night. The ghostly apparition of a man dressed in black, believed by some to be Saintsbury, has been seen sat astride a horse in the cellar. The spectre is often accompanied by a woman whose identity is unknown.

It may also be the ghost of Saintsbury who occasionally pops up in the bar and chats with customers. On several occasions, patrons have been surprised by a man wearing dark clothing and a tricorn hat who engages them in conversation only to suddenly disappear.

Guest Bedroom 4

Guest bedroom 4 is reputedly haunted by a woman dressed in white. She stands by the window gazing solemnly out onto Market Square below. Those who have seen her describe her gliding from the window then passing through a wall directly behind the bed. Who she is, and why she should haunt room 4 is a mystery. Some say she may be the ghost of a woman who became trapped and perished during a fire in the early 1700s.

The apparition in room 4 has allegedly seen off several guests who left in the middle of the night feeling utterly ghastly. Some complained of stomach cramps and nausea, but most disturbing are those who claim to have felt a pressure about their throats as if being strangled. I must say that when my partner and I visited room 4 I personally felt nothing out of the ordinary. My partner, however, felt decidedly cold even though the radiators were on maximum.

The current proprietors, Mike and Yvonne Wright, took over the hotel in March 2009 and were blissfully unaware of the Black Swan's reputation as one of England's most haunted establishments. But it wasn't long before they realised they were at the centre of a paranormal hotspot for ghothunters. The following is a quote from Mrs Wright from the *Gazette and Herald* on 23 April 2009:

> So many people have been phoning up about doing late night vigils, we agreed to continue them. Last week we had a group in from 11pm to 4.30am. Most of the time was spent in the cellar but then we all visited room 4. One of the girls in the party said she felt a presence next to her. She reached out her hand and she said she felt it getting very hot. She was getting quite distressed so we turned the light on. Her hand was dripping with sweat. Michael Murphy, our daughter's partner, held a thermometer at the spot and it went up from 17 to 27.6 degrees Celsius as we watched. There was no heat source in the room. We just can't explain it.

A few days later a film crew making a documentary for Wadworth brewery in Devizes were offered room 4 but turned it down. Mrs Wright said: 'They said they had been on the filming of the TV programme *Most Haunted* when it visited the Black Swan a few years ago and they didn't want to spend the night in room 4.'

It has not discouraged others however, as Mr and Mrs Wright are now inundated with bookings for room 4. The Black Swan has become extremely popular over the years and gained notoriety for its plethora of hauntings. Teams of ghost hunters, physic researchers, mediums and the media have all held vigils here.

Should you visit the medieval market town of Devizes, then why not check into the Black Swan Hotel for your stay? If you are feeling particularly brave book room 4, though I strongly suggest you ring in advance.

The Old Bell Hotel, Malmesbury

The Old Bell Hotel is thought to be the oldest hotel in England. It stands adjacent to the abbey, which is now in ruin. Many of the mysterious goings-on in the hotel occur in the east wing, which coincidentally was built on part of the former abbey churchyard. Several sarcophagi are rumoured to be concealed beneath the bar, although no excavation work has ever been carried out to confirm this. There has been an inn of sorts occupying the site as far back as AD 1220 and so, with everything else, it is hardly surprising that The Old Bell Hotel has built up quite a haunted reputation.

In the restaurant hangs a portrait of a woman dressed in grey. Is it by chance that this portrait bears a striking resemblance to that of the Grey Lady who is said to haunt the James Ody Room? Many guests claim to have witnessed her melancholy figure glide silently through the wall on one side of the room to the other. They are amazed, when later discussing their encounter with staff, to then be shown the portrait with the question, 'Is this the lady you saw?'

The Old Bell Hotel, Malmesbury, where furniture tends to have a mind of its own.

The Grey Lady's identity is a mystery but some say she was the victim of an abusive, unhappy marriage. Why this should cause her to haunt the hotel is anybody's guess. It is said that repeating the words 'Grey Lady' three times outloud within the James Ody Bedroom will make her appear.

Residents of the Danvers Room have reported seeing objects mysteriously levitate of their own accord, only to be hurled against the wall. Other residents claim their bedclothes have been pulled off in the dead of night, whilst others have complained to hotel staff that the contents of their bags have been emptied and left in disarray.

One of the most baffling accounts took place outside the bedroom door of the Foe Room. The guests had just checked in but when they arrived at the door of their room and inserted the key they could not gain access. Although the door could be unlocked it would only open a fraction and even the staff gave up trying to budge it. Eventually a ladder was fetched and propped up beneath the bedroom window outside, which had to be smashed open to gain entry. Once inside, the staff member was stunned to see that a heavy wooden wardrobe had been manoeuvred against the door. If this had been done as a prank by a guest or staff member then it would have meant climbing out of the window, securing it from the outside and then dropping from the first floor in full view of passers-by. I find that a little unlikely.

The night staff have also reported odd sounds and cold spots near the salon bar during their nightly rounds. Some are convinced they were being followed.

King & Queen, Highworth

The ancient hilltop town of Highworth stands overlooking the Thames valley. Archaeologists have uncovered finds from the Mesolithic, Neolithic, Bronze Age, Roman and Saxon eras, indicating

The King & Queen, Highworth, haunted by an executed monk.

the area has been occupied for at least 4,000 years. Highworth's strategic position was utilised as a Royalist stronghold during the English Civil Wars, only to be seized and occupied by Sir Thomas Fairfax in 1645, an occupation which coincided with a crippling outbreak of plague.

The King & Queen inn was granted an English Heritage Grade II listed status on 26 January 1955 and estimates vary as to this former coaching inn's age. While there is a date-stone marking its completion in 1677, there are some who speculate the pub's foundations are built over the remains of a monastery dating back some 500 years or so.

A little way down the high street from the King & Queen stands The Old Monastery (there appears to be little evidence to support the building was ever a monastery though) which was later renamed The Old Manor House, now converted into houses and flats numbering 1–4. Number 4 is a sixteenth-century structure which stands in front of an even older building believed to be fifteenth century or earlier. This building is thought to be the site of Eastrop Manor, once owned by the de Mendevilles, starting with the 1st Earl of Essex. The de Mandevilles continued to hold the Manor until 1361 when it was granted to the rector of Edington Priory. This association may go some way to support the existence of a monastery on one of the two sites, or indeed sandwiched between the two. It may also explain why the ghostly figure of a hunchbacked monk is seen inside and outside the King & Queen, walking along Market Square and the high street and in the church and crypt of St Michael and All Angels opposite. Tunnels (now blocked off) are said to run from the church crypt, beneath Market Square to the site of the old monastery close to the King & Queen.

The monk's story goes, that during the fourteenth century he was accused of breaking his vows of chastity, a crime punishable by death. It is believed, though not certain, that before the King & Queen became a coaching inn it was used as a courthouse. It is difficult to establish whether the monk's trial and subsequent execution were a result of sentencing passed on these premises. That aside, the poor chap is said to have been led outside and hanged in the courtyard adjacent to the pub. It is here where his ghost is most often seen.

There have been many sightings of the monk, one such encounter by a former landlord. He was woken in the dead of night by one of his dogs, who would normally sleep undisturbed outside his bedroom door. On this night, however, the animal was whimpering and growling. Puzzled, the landlord got out of bed to see what all the fuss was about. Having opened the bedroom door, he found his dog crouched low and trembling, with its hackles raised. It was staring fixedly in the direction of the courtyard where a second dog was tethered. Fearing an intruder, the landlord cautiously made his way downstairs accompanied by his reluctant companion. Quietly opening the door to the courtyard, he stepped outside to find his other dog backed up against a wall and in a similar state of anxiety, staring at something in the distance. Following the animal's gaze, he saw a figure at the end of the courtyard, bathed in moonlight and standing quite motionless. He would later describe the figure as 'hooded, dressed in white robes and appeared to be disfigured as if it had a hunched back'. 'Who's there?' he demanded. The figure remained unmoving and unresponsive, despite facing him. At this the landlord let loose his dogs, who refused to budge an inch. At that same moment the figure turned and glided silently across the courtyard toward the old stables block where it passed through a solid brick wall. Immediately after the apparition vanished, the animals calmed down and began tentatively sniffing at the spot where it had disappeared.

At a time when the gents' toilets were situated outside just off the courtyard, it was not unusual for patrons to dash back into the pub, all colour drained from their faces claiming to have come face to face with the monk.

The monk is not confined to the courtyard. His ghost has been seen walking the length of the bar and rising up through the floor at the spot where the old tunnels are said to be located. Heavy footsteps have been heard in the attic, though nobody ever goes up there, and in the corridor above the bar, which could have once led to the courtrooms. A frightening case several years ago saw glasses exploding on the bar-top and prompted one landlord to take out an insurance against claims for injury and shock as a result of encountering the ghost.

In the church of St Michaels opposite, a white robed and hooded figure has been seen at the alter and walking up the aisle, making its exit through the west door and out into the street where the monastery is thought to have stood. His ghost has also been spotted in Vicarage Lane immediately outside the church.

The Muddy Duck, Monkton Farleigh

This quaint seventeenth-century inn near Bath, formerly The King's Arms, is currently under the proprietorship of Simon Blagden and Vince Hanley (or at least it was when I went there last). Since taking over, Simon and Vince have spent a lot of time lovingly restoring and refurbishing the interior, although great care has been taken by both to retain many of its original features. Mr Hanley admits that since he and Mr Blagden took over the inn, they have become quite accustomed to the ghostly activity and were not surprised to learn that the pub has gained a reputation for being the most haunted inn in Wiltshire.

Most frequent are the disturbances immediately above the main bar, where heavy footsteps are sometimes heard walking the length of the upper floor and stopping by a window, at which point the muffled sobs of a woman can be perceived. These ghosts are never seen, but it is thought they may also be responsible for the strange goings in the bar below, where glasses are moved, lights are switched on and off and objects go missing.

The Muddy Duck, Monkton Farleigh, a monk and a miner are said to haunt this seventeenth-century inn.

The Black Monk

The oldest part of The Muddy Duck is believed to have been built by the monks in 1090, as somewhere they could officiate and administer the Farleigh estate. A priory, built about 1150, was dedicated to St Mary Magdalene and stood about 0.25 miles from the inn. Today, a Grade I listed Tudor Manor House occupies the site where the priory once stood and some of the material from the priory went to construct the house. The cellars are original to the priory, as are two partly restored thirteenth-century mullion windows. An adjoining shed contains twelfth- and thirteenth-century carved fragments including a coffin lid, a carved cross and sepulchre slabs. To the east of the house are two stone coffins thought to be part of the priory chapel. Several hundred yards from the house is a holy well, blessed by the monks and now enclosed by a thirteenth-century stone shelter. This is named the Monk's Conduit and still supplies fresh spring water to the manor and some of the cottages in the village.

It is not certain how the Black Monk met his demise. He was discovered by his brethren quite dead and slumped over paperwork in what is now the inn's main bar. On examination, no foul play was suspected and there is no record of cause of death. His body was moved and later buried. His ghost appears reluctant to rest though, for his black, hooded figure has been spotted walking slowly from the inn, to the Monk's Conduit where he passes through a door and disappears.

Ghost Miner

The hills around Monkton Farleigh have been mined for Bath Stone for over 200 years. In 1881 mining moved underground for the rich deposits of iolite limestone, some of which went to modernize Buckingham Palace during the nineteenth century.

The Muddy Duck was often used to conduct hearings and inquiries. A hearing was held in the early nineteenth century following the death of a miner under suspicious circumstances. The presiding magistrate was unconvinced that the evidence presented by one eyewitness miner was a factual account of his colleague's demise. Following the hearing, the miner who had given evidence suddenly died and it is thought to be his ghost that walks from the mines to the inn door where it disappears. Could it be that even in death his ghost is cursed for eternity, to deliver the truth of what happened on that day to a hearing long since disbanded?

The lane immediately outside the inn is haunted by a local woman who was killed when her carriage collided with the inn. She was heading home late at night when her horse took fright and bolted. Terrified, the woman tried to regain control but tragedy was to follow. Nearing the inn, her carriage clipped a wall and overturned, killing her outright. Her untimely and abrupt exit from this life may account for the ghostly screams and the thunder of a horse's hooves heard in the lane on the approach to the inn.

During construction work in the 1990s to open up a fireplace in one of the bars, two mysterious gentlemen in dark suits called in. They approached the barmaid and curtly told her, 'No good will come of your work here.' Having issued their warning the two gentlemen abruptly disappeared, leaving the barmaid somewhat shaken.

Renovations continued to the fireplace regardless. A little later, whilst knocking through a wall behind the fireplace, a box was found containing a large heavy key. The key was inserted in every lock in the building but failed to fit any of them. This strange and tantalising artefact now hangs behind and above the main bar. As for the two men, they were never seen again.

6

OTHER

Debenhams of Salisbury

The Debenhams department store in Salisbury is said to be haunted by the ghost of Henry Stafford, 2nd Duke of Buckingham who was beheaded in Market Square on the 2 November 1483. He was accused and found guilty of treason against King Richard III and his execution took place immediately outside where Debenhams now stands.

The store was formerly the site of the Blue Bore inn, later to become The Saracens Head inn. It is said this is where Buckingham spent his last hours, locked in an attic room which

Debenhams department store, haunted by the cheeky duke.

is immediately above the Blue Bore Restaurant situated at the rear of the store.

In 1838 a report appeared in the *Salopian Journal* that drew attention to excavations under the yard at the Saracens Head inn, at the point where Stafford was said to have been executed. A skeleton had been unearthed missing its head and right arm, and a slapdash examination by some of the locals claimed the remains must be those of Henry Stafford simply because of where it was found.

However, an insertion in the *Chronicle of the Grey Friars of London* states, 'Thys yere the duke of Buckyngham was be-heddyd at Salsbery, and is burryd at the Gray freres [in Salisbury].' This is most probably accurate as Richard III was known for treating his executed opponents with an honourable burial; he may have afforded Buckingham a similar privilege, putting him at Grey Friars and not under the backyard of the Saracens Head.

Wherever Stafford has been laid it would appear that his spirit is anything but resting, for his ghost has been seen in the sportswear department and the cheeky chappy also has a habit of popping into the lady's changing rooms where he is quite partial to 'hissing' at its occupants. He has also been spotted walking from the attic to a small enclosed yard at the back of the store.

Some years ago, a telephone engineer was working alone in the attic when he felt a cold hand grasp his shoulder. He fled the attic vowing never to return and someone else had to go back to retrieve his tools.

The hauntings are a ghost hunter's dream because they are so frequent. They are so well known that the Duke of Buckingham's ghost has been renamed 'The Duke of Debenhams'.

The ghost of a little girl in Victorian dress is said to haunt the area immediately outside the store, where she will happily greet visitors with a curtsey then show them to the entrance. At this point she vanishes.

Wiltshire's Highwaymen

Following the end of the Civil Wars, the threat of the highwaymen came into being. Many of them were discharged soldiers facing poverty due to lack of work. Already proficient horsemen and well adept in the use of firearms, these rouges preyed on the rich pickings available from the many coaches that passed through Devizes, Chippenham and Beckhampton on their way to London or Bath.

The thickly wooded Wiltshire countryside proved ideal cover for ambushing unwary travellers. During the eighteenth century it became popular for the London elite to spend their vacations in fashionable Bath where they would 'take the waters' at the Roman baths. Highwaymen used this annual pilgrimage to take advantage of the wealthy.

In general, highwaymen treated their victims with some courtesy, in fact they became known as 'Gentlemen of the Road'. Violence was rare unless you were foolish enough to provoke them. The best course of action was to hand over your lolly as quickly as you could, then just watch your valuables disappear into the woodland.

One of the most infamous groups of highwaymen in Wiltshire was the Cherhill Gang. These individuals operated on the tracks between Marlborough, Calne, Beckhampton and Devizes. To avoid identification and instill even more fear into their victims (if that were at all possible) the gang would strip naked and paint themselves white before attacking. I can only assume that they thought the eyes of their victims would be preoccupied somewhere other than their faces, ensuring some uncertainty when asked who had attacked them. A painting of the Cherhill Gang hangs in the Black Horse pub, between Beckhampton and Calne on the A4, the old London road.

Highwaymen became less common in the early part of the nineteenth century. Woodland was being cleared for agriculture, therefore diminishing much-needed cover for ambushing and the police presence was growing, the byways now frequently patrolled by armed officers. The Justice Offices also refused to grant licences to innkeepers who they believed were harbouring criminals and there was a growing availability of honest work, a route taken by many highwaymen to avoid the gallows.

The Ghost of Walter Leader

On the A361 between Beckhampton and Devizes stand two sarsen stones; a headstone and a footstone. They are said to mark the final resting place of Walter Leader, the unfortunate character who in 1811 was convicted and later hanged for his alleged involvement in the murder of Henry Castles. Castles was the driver of the ill-fated Royal Mail coach which was attacked and robbed by a gang of highwaymen, possibly the notorious Cherhill Gang. When the gang had completed their pernicious deed, they made off in the direction of Beckhampton, taking with them the loot and leaving Castles fatally wounded.

As they fled the scene they came across the decidedly drunk Walter Leader. Seizing the opportunity to frame someone for their crime, they attacked him and rendered him unconscious. Quickly returning to the scene of the crime, they dumped the incapacitated Walter next to Castles. Great care was then taken to incriminate him by placing a pistol in his hand. Leader was later discovered in this rather compromising situation and was promptly arrested. At his trial the evidence against him seemed insurmountable and Leader was sentence to hang for the murder of Henry Castles, probably at nearby Cherhill or Morgan's Hill, both infamous for public hangings and their gruesome gibbets.

It is said that as Leader was being lead to the gallows he saw a horseman approaching in the distance and pleaded with his executioners to wait in case he may be pardoned at the last moment. They didn't and Walter Leader was duly dispatched. Minutes after his death the horseman arrived and demanded Leader's reprieve. As it turned out, one of the gang members had got into a quarrel with the others and decided to turn 'King's Evidence' at Bath. A horseman had been dispatched with orders to relinquish Leader from his crime, unfortunately arriving a tad too late.

Leader's body was duly cut down and carried by cart to where the A361 cuts through the landscape. He was buried face-down, with his head to the west on a spot marked by the two sarsen stones. His grave lies where the old Roman road crosses the A361 a mile west of Beckhampton.

People still report seeing the ghostly figure of a man wearing a black cloak and a tricorn hat wandering the adjacent byways. A similar figure has been seen close to where the gibbet once stood at Cherhill. Could these apparitions be that of Walter Leader?

Two sarsen stones near Beckhampton are thought to mark the final resting place of Walter Leader.

Devizes Castle

The first castle to be built in Devizes was constructed around 1080 by Osmond, Bishop of Salisbury. Osmond's castle was a motte-and-bailey affair with a wooden three-storey tower set high on a palisade mound. The outer bailey would have included a defensive ditch, stockade and drawbridge. The castle was often used to secure prisoners of state such as Robert Duke of Normandy, incarcerated for twenty years following a lengthy dispute with his younger brother Henry I.

After fire destroyed the castle in 1113, work to rebuild it was undertaken by Viceroy Bishop Roger of Caen who lavished a huge amount of money on its construction. Built primarily of stone this time, the new castle would have had a keep, castellated walls, a portcullis and a very deep moat. Its banked sides are still visible today.

The castle was badly damaged again in 1645 by repeated assaults from Cromwell's army, who eventually seized it. An order was issued from parliament to have the castle 'slighted', a term used to initiate dismantling. Very little remains now, though parts of the keep were discovered during the nineteenth century when the Leach family began work constructing a new castle in a Neo-Norman Gothic style. They added towers to the south and north with castellated walls and an impressive gatehouse with double-grid-patterned timber gates set into a large Norman archway.

Over its colourful history the castle has gained a reputation for being haunted; a mysterious woman dressed in white has been seen countless times wandering the corridors. Originally she was thought to be Lady Isabella, daughter of Charles VI of France. The story goes that, unhappy in a turbulent, politically arranged marriage to King Richard II of England, Isabella sought the attentions of another man. She was often left alone in the castle and it was during one of these solitary episodes that she met and fell in love with a young knight. The king was told of her infidelity and the knight was duly arrested and put to death. But Isabella's fate was even more gruesome. She was to be buried alive within the castle walls on the orders of her jealous husband.

Devizes Castle, where some dogs fear to tread.

In reality Isabella's forced marriage in 1396 was at the tender age of 6, so the likelihood of her engaging in a relationship with another man would have been extremely slim. Not only that, but it is well documented that she returned to France aged 11 after King Richard, returning from a military campaign in Ireland, was imprisoned and mysteriously murdered. It is also true that, though their marriage was arranged in an effort to calm the tensions between England and France, they each carried a deep respect for the other. Therefore, the true identity of 'The Lady in White' remains a tantalising mystery.

Another of the castle's ghosts is that of a Cavalier who haunts the main staircase. He is described as very tall and seems always to be in a rush as he dashes down the stairs with his sword clattering at his side. Story has it that one elderly resident, while making her way up to her bedroom, was suddenly confronted by the Cavalier as he dashed past leaving her in his icy wake. Another resident similarly climbing the stairs was abruptly subjected to an icy blast as the apparition materialised immediately in front of him and then proceeded to pass right through him.

A man's voice has been heard coming from one of the bedrooms. During the Second World War the castle was used as a barracks and the story goes that one soldier was inclined to sleepwalk. This meant he was forever waking the others. A decision was made to confine him to one bedroom where he was locked in at night. People who have stayed in that room have been woken by the sound of someone murmuring and a shuffling sound, as if someone is moving about the room. I'm inclined to think that whatever is haunting that room must surely not be that same soldier, I can't believe that his comrades would have locked him in and left him for dead no matter how irritating his sleepwalking was.

Probably the most eerie and most active of the castle's ghosts is that of an elderly woman who has been seen in the gallery. She is dressed in nineteenth-century 'widows weeds', a garment worn during a time of mourning. She walks with a stoop whilst grasping a walking stick. There is something a little disturbing about her presence and for that matter the gallery in general. Over the years a number of dogs have refused to enter the room, instead preferring to stand transfixed whilst growling at something that only they can sense.

Today the castle is privately owned and not accessible to the public, but there are still impressive views to be seen from the castle car park at the rear of Market Square.

Old Wardour Castle

Old Wardour Castle is situated near Antsy Tisbury, on the A30 south-west of Salisbury. Now just a ruin, this dazzling-white, stone, hexagonal castle stands majestically amidst the Wiltshire countryside as a reminder of fourteenth-century French-inspired architecture. It was built by John Lovel, 5th Lord Lovel, in 1393, primarily as a fortification but later became a lavish and slightly decadent country home. In 1547 Sir Thomas Arundell of Cornwall purchased the castle, which remained the property of the Arundells until its destruction during the English Civil War.

Old Wardour Castle, a tranquil ruin with a Civil War haunting.

The castle was badly damaged in the seventeenth century during a twenty-five-day siege by Cromwell's army. With her husband away, Lady Blanche Arundell fought valiantly with just a handful of men and close family friends to keep Cromwell's Roundheads from the castle door. Ultimately, realising they faced defeat from superior weaponry and also because food and supplies were running low, Lady Arundell surrendered. One story goes that the terms of her surrender were not honoured and she and her party were taken prisoner and then executed. However, there is strong evidence that she left Wardour with honour and died at Winchester on 28 October 1649 and was buried alongside her husband in Tisbury.

The ghost of Lady Blanche Arundell still haunts the ruins and grounds. She is often seen walking from the castle to the nearby lake at dusk; mainly alone but occasionally accompanied by others, perhaps those who fought with her. The castle has been host to many paranormal vigils, some parties reporting an overwhelming feeling of calm when inside the ruin which is surprising when one considers its violent history. The English Heritage staff who I spoke to at great length during my visit, told me of several accounts where staff and visitors have experienced a feeling of being watched whilst in the castle and grounds, some even claiming to have seen the ghostly apparition of Lady Arundell.

The castle stands in the grounds of New Wardour House, which was built in the eighteenth century by the Arundell family who decided the castle should be left as a folly. They hired the famous architect Lancelot 'Capability' Brown to landscape the gardens and lakes which are preserved to this day. The castle remains a beautiful and romantic vista, and should you venture into the woodland at the rear of the ticket booth you will more than likely discover a modern stone circle and grotto, just two of many little diversions along the way.

For the film and music buffs amongst you, you may like to know the castle was the backdrop during the filming of certain scenes for the movie *Robin Hood, Prince of Thieves* back in the 1990s, and a photograph taken inside the castle was used for the cover of Sting's album, *Ten Summoner's Tales*.

Following the death of the last Lord Arundell in 1944, the castle passed to the state. It is now owned by English Heritage and the new house remains a private residence.

Devizes Town Hall and the Old Town Lock-up

One of the most haunted buildings in Devizes has to be the town hall and its lock-up, situated in St Johns Street. The town hall was rebuilt in 1806 by Thomas Baldwin, City Architect of Bath. Originally the site was occupied by the old Wool Hall, (*c.* 1615) and before that the Tudor Yarn Hall (*c.* 1575). The old town lock-up is situated at the rear of the building and was in use from the early fifteenth century until the early nineteenth century. It still has its original metal door.

Lock-ups were commonly built of stone and were usually circular with a domed stone roof and a single slit in one wall. Very often they would have had a set of stocks immediately outside where those under restraint could be publicly humiliated. Passers-by would be encouraged to throw anything from rotten eggs to excrement at those being punished. Devizes lock-up is different as it is integral to the town hall building and is similar in construction to a conventional cellar. It has three chambers with a stone fireplace at one end and a flight of steps that lead up to street level. It is a dark, damp, brooding and inhospitable place, certainly not somewhere to spend a night alone (unless you are a ghost hunter that is).

Lock-ups were used to detain people who were causing an affray, more often than not drunks and brawlers. These individuals would be locked up overnight by the duty turnkey or watchman then either released or brought before a magistrate the following day for sentencing, depending on the severity of their crime. A sentence could be anything from a fine to a lengthy prison term and in some cases the gallows. Many of those sentenced to death would spend their last night on earth incarcerated in a lock-up, and Devizes was no exception.

A group of school children went on a guided tour of the building, the last stop of which was the spooky lock-up. The children had just seated themselves on an old church pew procured from St James church nearby, when one of the teachers noticed a boy staring intently into one corner of the cellar. When asked what he was looking at he replied, 'The man in the corner Miss!' She looked but saw nothing. Understandably the boy became quite agitated and had to be led out.

Devizes lock-up is a hotspot for paranormal investigators and vigils are often held here with some surprising results. There is an atmosphere about the place created, I shouldn't wonder, by these chambers on occasion being used as cells for the condemned. The human torment foremost in the minds of those waiting to die at the gallows must have been intense, intense enough to possibly leave a lasting imprint or residue forever etched into the fabric of these cold stone walls.

Devizes Town Hall and its infamous lock-up, said to be haunted by the souls condemned here.

For the condemned there would be a short trip to Market Square or Gallows Ditch to the rear of Devizes Castle on Hillworth Road (the latter is now a small area of green on the edge of a housing estate). This area is also a magnet for paranormal investigators, ghost hunters and dowsers. I have participated in some dowsing along with a group of ghost hunters, but have to admit I was a tad sceptical. Whilst I walked slowly across the green there was one spot where my dowsing rods behaved in a most curious manner, by crossing and uncrossing as I stepped into then out of this one spot. I have no explanation as to why this should have happened and I still remain unconvinced. There are parts of the green where some folk have felt strong emotional connections; feelings of foreboding, fear and nausea are not uncommon.

In the town hall itself there are several locations that make some staff feel uncomfortable, especially when alone. Carole Berry, our guide for the morning, was kind enough to show my partner and I around the building, pointing out those rooms which some staff have felt a strong presence in. There was the ballroom, where on occasion Carole has felt she was not entirely alone, as if someone were standing close behind her, and the grand jury room, where sentences were handed out to the town's miscreants (again this room seems to exude a presence, an inexplicable feeling of being watched). Carole would not enter the minstrel gallery alone, as she has experienced tightness in her chest and difficulty in breathing there. The room overlooks the ballroom via a curtain and is a little claustrophobic, so it is easy to see why some may be affected by the confines of such a small space. The entrance to the elevator, which is situated at the end of a short corridor, has also been described as exuding a malevolent presence.

It is not for me to draw conclusions as to why some staff feel unease in certain rooms; I'm sure their experiences were very real. Having said that, I believe that the mind can play tricks – how often have we heard that. We are social animals, our lives depend greatly on contact with others, and so for some just being alone can cause unease. It is during this isolation that the mind may compensate for solitude by fabricating another presence to fill the void, whether good or bad, usually the latter. For some, being alone can make us vulnerable and nervous, a state of mind not felt when in the company of those we know.

The Wiltshire Moonraker Legend

The location of the famous 'Wiltshire Moonraker' legend is believed to be the Crammer pond, Devizes. The Crammer first appeared in Dore's map of Devizes in 1759, originally called the Kramer after the German merchants who used to erect stalls beside the pond to sell their wares. It was also a popular stop-off point for drovers to water their cattle before moving onto Devizes market.

The legend goes that in 1791 a group of smugglers based close by in Bishops Cannings had hidden contraband brandy in the Crammer. Their presence at the Crammer on one particular moonlit night had drawn the attention of a team of excise men, who had been tipped off that something untoward was going on near the pond. Taking cover nearby, the excise men waited patiently for their quarry. In due course the smugglers arrived and began pawing at the surface of the pond with what appeared to be rakes. Unknown to the excise men, the smugglers had also been tipped off and had hatched a cunning plan.

The Wiltshire Moonraker legend. (© Christine Bozier)

Seeing enough and with their suspicions aroused, the excise men broke cover and quickly confronted the smugglers enquiring as to their business. The smugglers played dumb and said they were from Bishops Cannings and were 'rakin' in that gurt yaller cheese in yonder pond,' which briefly translates; 'we are trying to get that great yellow cheese out of the pond.'

Hearing their explanation, the excise men believed these rogues to be simpletons from the village of Bishops Cannings (a village that had acquired a reputation for more than its fair share of fools over the years, becoming the butt of many jokes) so were inclined to believe their ridiculous story. Satisfied they had just encountered several idiots attempting to rake in a reflection of the moon thinking it to be a giant cheese, they rode off. Little did they know the village idiots had just had the last laugh. It is said that on some nights when the moon is full and it casts a silvery path across the pond, those same smugglers still rake at its reflection.

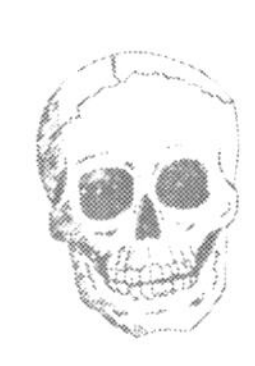

BIBLIOGRAPHY

Books

Dobson, Margaret and Simone Brightstein, *Hosts of Ghosts* (Wiltshire: Ex Libris Press, 1998)

Matthews, Rupert, *Haunted Places of Wiltshire* (Countryside Books: Berkshire, 2004)

Wiltshire, Kathleen, *Ghosts & Legends of the Wiltshire Countryside* (Compton Russell: Salisbury, 1973)

Underwood, Peter, *Ghosts of Wiltshire* (Ilkley: Bossiney Books, 1989)

Spencer, John and Anne, *The Ghost Handbook* (New York: Macmillan, 1998)

Guidebooks

National Trust
English Heritage

Websites

www.britainexpress.com
www.british-history.ac.uk
www.english-heritage.org.uk
www.gazetteandherald.co.uk/news/towns/devizesheadlines
www.nationaltrust.org.uk
www.paranormaldatabase.com
www.thepeerage.com
www.timetravel-britain.com
www.wikipedia.org

Lightning Source UK Ltd.
Milton Keynes UK
UKOW04f1330150114

224612UK00004B/17/P